FOR LADIES ONLY?

EVE'S FILM REVIEW:
PATHE CINEMAGAZINE 1921-33

Jenny Hammerton

Number ten in a series of monographs
on precinema and silent film

**THE
PROJECTION BOX**

With special thanks to Vic and my parents,

to whom this book is dedicated

Published in association with
British Pathe plc

Text © Jenny Hammerton, 2001
All illustrations © British Pathe plc.
except where stated

ISBN 1 903000 02 5

A CIP catalogue record for this publication is available from
the British Library

Published by The Projection Box
12 High Street Hastings East Sussex TN34 3EY
s-herbert@easynet.co.uk

Printed by Windmill Press, Uckfield, East Sussex
Typeset by David Brown, Maynards Green, East Sussex

CONTENTS

Acknowledgements

Although this is only a slim volume, there are many people I would like to thank for their support and guidance – it might be the only chance I ever get in print! I am lucky to include many of the following as friends as well as colleagues, so a big thank you to:

Stephen Herbert, Mo Heard, David Cleveland, Jane Alvey, Luke McKernan, Ron Saunders, Vic Pratt, Lawrence Napper, Gary Chapman, Hugh Purcell, Suzanne Philips, Sarah Broughton, Andrew Higson, Charles Barr, Pam Cook, Laraine Porter, Tony Fletcher, Nick Hiley, Phill Walkley, Neil Brand, Cy Young, Fred Lake, Jerry Kuehl, Ronald Grant, John Eve, Thierry Rolland, Serge Viallet, Tom Gunning, Annette Kuhn, Janet Moat, Julia Parker, David Francis, Jim Ballantyne, Adele Carrol, Liz Turner, Carolyn Faber, Cheri Pugh, James A. Smith, Christine Broadbridge, Heather Temple, Chippie Hudson, Wayne Garvie, Alf Penn, Tracey Stephenson, Gary Long, Mike Hudson, Margaret Mary Hollins, Ruth Andrew, Katy Dugdale, Steph Waters, Phil Snoswell, Maria O'Donnell, Rachael Holdsworth, Katy Sinka, David Hallam, Caroline Frick, Rachel Healy, Jane Paul, Richard McGrath, Claire Fox, Sarah Lee, Sanja Adamovic, Amelia Hamer, Emma Binns, Howard Gordon, Mark Davis, Margaret Kirby, Julian Aston, Peter Fydler, Julian Del Guidice, all my colleagues at British Pathe and staff at the following institutions: ScreenSound Australia, the New Zealand Film Archive, Pathé Archives in Paris, the British Film Institute National Film and Television Archive, the Newspaper Library at Colindale, and the Amersham Public Library.

Jenny Hammerton
London, July 2001

1 – Three Girls in a Boat : An Introduction

When I first heard about *Eve's Film Review* it was the titles that tantalised. *Costumes for the Peaches on the Beaches, Eve Dresses her Tresses* and *That Trouser Complex* are just three of the examples that whetted my appetite. David Cleveland of the East Anglian Film Archive is wholly to blame for my obsession with a collection of obscure but fascinating films. For it was he who showed me *Three Girls in a Boat* – a beautiful short film featuring three dolly birds on holiday on the Norfolk Broads. They swab the decks, brush their hair and drink cups of tea as their pleasure boat cruises through the county's waterways. I was intrigued by this two and a half minute film. It was not a news item; nothing much happened. Neither was it an advertising film; the designer of the girls' outfits was not named. David informed me that it was a segment from a Pathe cinemagazine. I was none the wiser.

I decided to find out more and was directed to the British Universities Film and Video Council poster which lists newsreels and cinemagazines produced in Britain from the early 1900s. My eyes were magically drawn to a line nestling between entries for *Fox News* and the *Empire News Bulletin*. 'Eve's Film Review – 1921 to 28th December 1933 – Cinemagazine for women audiences.' If I had been a character in a cartoon strip, a light bulb would have appeared above my head. From the Archive it was a short jaunt to the University library and the microfiche copies of the Slade Film Register listings of newsreel and cinemagazine item titles.[1] *The Coquettish Mantilla – and How to Wear It, That Powder Puff, Introducing Miss Tea Cosy, A While You Wait Frock, Are Women's Sports Too Strenuous?* My eyes boggled at the sight of all these titles and more. Could the films be as good as they sounded? The short answer is yes. The long answer is held partly within the pages of this book, and mostly within the film vaults of British Pathe and other archives around the world.

This book has grown from the dissertation I wrote for my Masters in Film Archiving at the University of East Anglia in 1994. Ron Saunders allowed me to view around 200 *Eve's Film Review* items at Pathe's Pinewood Studios office, and I realised that the films were even more fabulous than their titles suggested. Glorious fashions, bizarre beauty regimes, quirky home crafts, and astounding cabaret acts were amongst the treats in store. After completing the archiving course my fascination with the films endured. In 1996 I was invited to join Pathe to catalogue their silent cinemagazines and felt like the luckiest woman alive. The collection of almost 1500 *Eve's Film Review* items is now fully catalogued, but my interest in the films continues to grow.

Pathe embarked on a large digitisation and recataloguing project in the year 2000. It is the company's intention to make its entire collection viewable over the internet in the next few years. Until then Pathe have made a selection of *Eve's Film Review* items available to view at www.britishpathe.com/all_about_eve.htm (see appendix 4 which lists the viewable items). Full descriptions of catalogued *Eve's Film Review* items are available through Pathe's searchable database at www.britishpathe.com

Pathe's Holdings

Pathe's surviving *Eve's Film Review* material is held in a collection of 313 cans known as the 'Eve Pics'. This name is an amalgamation of the 'Eve' of *Eve's Film Review* and the 'Pic' of *Pathe Pictorial*, Pathe's other silent cinemagazine. There are around 2600 individual films in the Eve Pic collection, roughly 1500 of them being *Eve's Film Review* items, while most of the others are silent *Pathe Pictorial* items. It has taken almost three years to view each film, describe the contents in a database record, and check for signs of decomposition. This project was set in motion by Pathe to make the collection more accessible to film researchers, and to identify those films which needed to be copied to safety stock for preservation purposes. There is a strong possibility that other *Eve's Film Review* items will be found erroneously stored within other parts of the Pathe collection, but the majority of silent cinemagazine items held by Pathe are now catalogued. Many of the early *Eve's Film Review* items are 'missing believed lost'; only approximately 50% of the films made survive at Pathe. I have compiled a list of those titles I know to be missing from the Pathe collection and this forms Appendix 3. It is impossible to compile a comprehensive list as Pathe's issue sheets are incomplete, but the list serves as a guide. Some *Eve's Film Review* items are held at the National Film and Television Archive, at the Library of Congress, and in other national and regional film archives and private collections. I would be pleased to hear from anyone who finds any of the films on the 'missing' list as I am compiling a record of holdings other than those at Pathe.

Nomenclature

During the early days of my research into *Eve's Film Review*, friends assumed that I was referring to a film critique presented by a woman called Eve. Part of the problem was the use of the word 'review' which has changed in meaning since the 1920s. In the period under consideration 'review' was used interchangeably with the rather more evocative 'revue'. Described in the dictionary as a 'theatrical

(1) Frame from an opening sequence of an Eve's Film Review *issue, c1928*

(2) Alternative title sequence Eve and Everybody's Film Review, *c1921*

entertainment ... comprising many unrelated episodes', 'revue' seems more apt to describe the cinemagazine. The name of Eve was used in the 1920s to symbolise 'everywoman', just as Adam might suggest 'everyman'. Thus the name *Eve's Film Review* would have suggested to the cinema audience that this was a revue style entertainment directed at women.

Eve's Film Review was sometimes also known as *Eve Pictorial* and *Eve and Everybody's Film Review*. As far as I can ascertain, in the 1920s and early 1930s the name *Eve Pictorial* was an unofficial term used within Pathe to differentiate the films from *Pathe Pictorial* productions. The name was occasionally used by contemporary critics but the reel was never officially called *Eve Pictorial*.[2] Sometimes the reel took on the name *Eve and Everybody's Film Review* acknowledging the fact that films could appeal to both male and female cinemagoers. However, from my research the use of this longer name doesn't seem to be accompanied by any alteration of thematic scope or tone of address. Trade journals referred to the cinemagazine as *Eve's Film Review* until its demise, and title cards for each item continued to bear the name *Eve's Film Review* although some opening sequences featured the longer title: **1** and **2**. For simplicity I have referred to the reel as *Eve's Film Review* throughout.[3]

Cinemagazines, Screen Magazines, Interest Films
The term 'cinemagazine' was used from the late 1910s to describe a cinematic diversion similar to the newsreel in format but very different both in subject matter and tone of address. Cinemagazines were produced weekly and offered a 'slice of life', containing films showing the strange and curious as well as the workaday. Within this book I will attempt to clarify the boundaries of the cinemagazine, compare it to the newsreel, and investigate its standing as a form which lies outside the conventions of the narrative form which has come to dominate cinema screens.

Contemporary reviews often used the term 'interest films' to cover both short documentary films about one particular subject, and cinemagazines. The phrase 'interest films' was sometimes used as a catchall term for non-narrative films which accompanied the feature. Cinemagazines are sometimes also referred to as 'screen magazines'. Again for reasons of clarity, I shall use the term cinemagazine throughout this book unless referred to in other terms by writers or within quotations.

The Silent Era
I use the expressions 'silent cinema' and 'the silent era' throughout this book with reservations. Recent work by film historians has dispelled many myths about the 'silence' of the early period. Of course, many films would have been

accompanied by pianists, or in large cinemas by a group of musicians. There was also much experimentation with sound technology before *The Jazz Singer* (1927) hit the screens. However, *Eve's Film Review* was produced without an accompanying soundtrack and continued to feature intertitles until its demise in 1933,[4] therefore it seems appropriate to study it in the context of 'silent cinema'.

Production Personnel

Although *Eve's Film Review* was ostensibly an entertainment created for women, it was made by men. An article in *The Film Renter and Moving Picture News* of 2 December 1922 lists the following cameramen as working on the *Pathe Pictorial*: Kenneth Gordon, Arthur Fisher and D. Tampieri. It is highly likely that these cameramen also worked on *Eve's Film Review,* Kenneth Gordon certainly did as there are several accounts of him filming for the series in the trade press.[5] Frederick Watts was the Editor of the reel, A.V. Curtice the Assistant Editor, and cartoonist and filmmaker Joe Noble was a regular contributor to the series. Montague Redknap and Arthur Farmer may also have worked as cameramen for *Eve's Film Review*. A man called John Edward Eve (known as Edward Eve) was working at Pathe during the 1920s, and according to his son was an ideas man and script writer. It is quite possible that Mr Eve was responsible for writing the intertitles which provide *Eve's Film Review* with much of its humour, and he probably suggested suitable subjects for inclusion in the cinemagazine. I will explore later the resonances of the use of the name 'Eve' during the period, and for now would suggest that it was a happy coincidence that Edward Eve was working on the series rather than it actually being named after him.[6]

In Pathe's paper records I have found reference to four women working under Fred Watts during the time *Eve's Film Review* was made, but I have been unable to ascertain their job roles. That the women (Miss Caley, Miss Ireland, Miss Smith and Miss Coundon) are only mentioned on the 'Late Sheets' (one of them getting a black mark for being only 2 minutes late for work!) suggests that they probably had somewhat lowly status within the company.

There was a vibrant trade in short cinemagazine films during the 1920s and 1930s. As well as allocating subject matter to the Pathe staff cameramen, Frederick Watts bought in material from freelance filmmakers around the world. As he proudly announced in 1928 of his two cinemagazines *Eve's Film Review* and *Pathe Pictorial*:

'The store from which we gather our subjects, is the world, and we search the world for our material. Very few spots on the globe are not visited at one time or another by the ubiquitous "PIC" Cameraman, or our Agents, whether on top of the highest mountain or deep below the sea.'[7]

The British branch of Pathe also exchanged many films with overseas divisions of the company, replacing foreign titles and intertitles to match the style of the British release. Pathe paperwork often states the source of the original film, and trade seemed particularly strong between the United States, Britain and France. The same story could thus be seen in several versions around the world. The British edition of *Eve's Film Review* was itself exported, being seen as far afield as Egypt, Australia and the West Indies; the reel was even screened aboard some ocean liners.

Pathé Frères

Like many companies, British Pathe has changed its name many times over the years. Originally Pathé Frères, then Pathé, then just Pathe. As I am writing today, the official name of the company is British Pathe plc. I will use the short Anglicised form 'Pathe' unless quoting from contemporary sources.

All About Eve

In this book I am celebrating the fact that glimpses of the kaleidoscopic world of female pleasures were captured on film over a twelve year period. That so many of these films survive is truly remarkable when so much material from the silent era has been 'lost'. By attempting to place the films within the context of women's lives during the period, by a consideration of the cinemagazine's relation to print magazines and through an illustration of the appeal these films might have to men as well as women, I hope to demonstrate what a unique and fascinating series *Eve's Film Review* was.

I recognise the difficulties involved in looking from a 21st century perspective at a product made in the 1920s and 1930s. In an attempt to contextualise the films, I have consulted newspapers and women's magazines from the 1920s and 1930s as well as film related publications of the time. The popularity of *Eve's Film Review* cannot be quantified by box office receipts, and contemporary reactions from audiences have been almost impossible to find. It is very difficult therefore to draw conclusions about how *Eve's Film Review* was received by audiences, but through a study of the 'text' of the cinemagazine and an exploration of the range of pleasures it offers, I hope to show the potential this series had to delight the audience of its time as well as the modern audience of today.

2 – The Arrival of the Women's Film
The Female Cinemagoer and the Full Supporting Programme

The Bioscope of 28 April 1921 announced a new cinematic attraction with the headline: 'The Arrival of the Women's Film. Pathes Present *Eve's Film Review*'. The article continued:

'Once again the enterprising firm of Pathé Frères is introducing an entirely new novelty into cinema programmes. The latest venture of the company is the production of a weekly film dealing in a novel and interesting manner with all matters of interest to women…

The film, which will be approximately 500 feet in length, will contain animated pictures of subjects essentially of interest to ladies. Exclusive fashion pictures, animated sidelights of society, music, art, sport and drama, will be included. Everything that appeals to the innate Eve in women will be covered by this feature, which in view of the large percentage of ladies who consistently patronise cinemas should supply a long-felt want.

Hints and advice on the domestic arts, such as cooking and dressmaking, will be shown. Peeps at famous stage stars in their dressing rooms, and women at work in novel and interesting occupations, are a few of the subjects which will be dealt with. The scope afforded by the feature will enable a varied and consistently interesting film of this nature to be produced each week. The first issue will be on June 9th.'

The Female Cinemagoer
When *Eve's Film Review* was launched in 1921, both film-makers and cinema proprietors had recognised the female cinemagoer as their principal audience. Contemporary writers such as Iris Barry observed that women substantially outnumbered men in cinema auditoriums in Britain in the twenties. She advised that '…one thing never to be lost sight of in considering the cinema is that it exists for the purpose of pleasing women. Three out of every four of all cinema audiences are women.'[1] In 1925, Marjory Williams had this to say: 'That women are the chief patrons of the kinema is a fact as patent as it is easy to explain. It is too often their only relaxation, their one chance of mental expansion.'[2]

Cinema owners believed that even if a woman was accompanied by her husband or family, she would make the decision which film to see and which cinema to visit. To lure such women to their particular picture palace, proprietors began to emphasise the comfort and luxuriousness of their establishments, offering pleasures supplementary to the moving picture programme including 'ladies' rest rooms', ballrooms and tea rooms. The Regent Cinema in Norwich, for example, stressed the virtues of its café in advertisements: 'The Social Centre for Light Refreshments, Dainty Teas, Cream Ices, Rest and Music is the Regent Lounge Cafe'.[3] That a large number of mothers with children visited the cinema at this time is evidenced by the fact that many proprietors offered space for them to leave their prams. Afternoon shows in particular were aimed at the female audience, hence the phenomenon of the 'matinee idol' such as Rudolph Valentino. Many cinema magazines were published, the majority of which were directed at the female audience and consequently were full of advertisements for beauty products, often endorsed by the stars of the screen.

Mike Hammond's work on cinemas in Southampton during the First World War shows that some cinema managers sought to attract large numbers of working women by consistently screening films with strong female heroines and 'Cinderella' storylines.[4] Film narratives of the early post war period continued to feature as their central characters working class girls 'who made good'. Wish fulfilment fantasies featuring shop girls or clerks who suddenly found fame, fortune or romance were extremely popular with young working women in the 1920s. Cinema offered an escape from the daily toil and women could imagine themselves in the place of their on-screen heroines. Interviewed about her cinemagoing experiences in 1926 one young woman probably expressed the views of many when she sighed: 'How I have longed to cast off the dulled shackles of today and step, free and proud and ecstatic, into that misty dream-world.'[5]

The Full Supporting Programme
In the 1920s cinemas offered a 'full supporting programme' to accompany the feature. Cinema managers were keen to offer their patrons value for money and cinemagoers would be treated to cartoons, short films, newsreels and cinemagazines in addition to the main attraction. Cinemagazines were issued weekly and during the twenties cinema proprietors had many to choose from including *Gaumont Mirror, British Screen Tatler, Ideal Cinemagazine,* and *Around the Town.* Amongst those on offer, *Eve's Film Review* was unique in that it was promoted as being specifically for the female audience.[6] The subjects that Pathe believed would interest women cinemagoers were listed in their publicity: **3.** These themes echoed the type of material found in women's print magazines of the day, with fashion being the driving force. Pathe had been producing short fashion films since the early 1910s, and a 1911 *Bioscope* review read as follows:

Pathé presents

EVE'S FILM REVIEW

THE WOMAN'S PICTURE.

Read these Contents of No. 1.

HIGH ART—VERY. A popular actress has a stork painted on her shapely shoulders by a well-known artist.

RENEE KELLY AT HOME. There's nothing quite so fascinating as seeing stage "stars" in the open air.

FOLDING SERVIETTES. A Hotel waiter shows how to create dainty shapes with serviettes.

M'LADY'S DRESS. Exclusive pictures of Ascot gowns by Paquin.

THE MINUET. Charming picture of the minuet dance in an old-world garden.

TITLE COMPETITION. £50 is offered for an accepted alternative title to Eve's Film Review suggested by a lady.

The first issue of this new, chic, film of feminity will be released on THURSDAY, JUNE 9th. Future issues will deal charmingly and comprehensively with the whole field of woman's activities in Fashion, Stage, Sport, Home and Boudoir. Your lady patrons will thank you for it every week.

PATHÉ FRÈRES CINEMA LTD., 84, Wardour Street, London, W.1 & Branches.

(3) Eve's Film Review *launch advertisement in* The Cinema *9 June 1921*

13

'The delight with which the coloured fashions in Pathé's Animated Gazette have been viewed by thousands of feminine spectators every week has been the precursor of a frequently expressed desire for films giving a greater number of pictures showing the changes foreshadowed by Dame Fashion. To meet this desire and demand for fashion films, Messrs. Pathé are commencing a series showing the coming models from Paris. The present one gives coloured pictures of hats, dinner gowns, tailor-made costumes, walking dresses, negligees and teagowns.'[7]

The fashion film continued to be popular with female cinemagoers and this must have been a deciding factor in Pathe's resolution to produce a weekly film specifically directed at women. That *Eve's Film Review* might encourage women to visit their establishment would have prompted exhibitors to promote the reel. Pathe produced glorious colour posters advertising the subject matter of the weekly women's film for cinema managers to display, which might have tempted passing trade or clinched the choice between two programmes: **4.**[8]

Flappers and Femininity

In defining female cinemagoers as the audience for *Eve's Film Review*, Pathe were influenced by many debates of the time about what it was to be a woman. In the early 1920s the mass media were full of discussion about working women and the possibility of universal suffrage. Women's magazines flourished at this time, and the post-war period saw a recognition of women as a lucrative new spending force for consumer goods. Advertisements for clothes and cosmetics accompanied features on the same subjects, creating a distinct feminine ideal. However, magazines also investigated new inroads women were making into traditionally masculine realms. The presentation of many contradictory ideas surrounding the idea of 'the modern woman' runs throughout *Eve's Film Review*, with many films contrasting the contemporary jazz baby with her old-fashioned grandmamma of yesteryear.[9]

Masculinity and femininity are terms involving many complex assumptions and culturally defined meanings. *Eve's Film Review* is a forum constantly referring to and attempting to define what it is to be feminine at a certain point in time, but of course femininity is not a universally static concept. Other societies with cultures radically different from our own have differing ideas about what it is to be feminine and what constitutes acceptable behaviour for women. Within British society, too, the idea of femininity is subject to fluctuation and change. During the period under consideration, assumptions about a 'woman's place' in society and about what constituted acceptable female behaviour were constantly being challenged. Changes in perceptions of women and femininity are documented throughout *Eve's Film Review*, as I hope to show. Throughout this

(4) Eve's Film Review *advertising poster*
(David Francis)

15

book I will be using the terms 'masculinity' and 'femininity' to refer to the notions generally held at the time *Eve's Film Review* was made, about what made women different from men. I do however recognise that not all women would have conformed to the feminine ideal of the time, and indeed many would not have wanted to.

Today the 1920s are summed up for many in the figure of the 'flapper', a young flighty woman who exhibits outrageous behaviour and a refined dress sense. Cigarette holders, bobbed haircuts, fringed dresses, cocktails, and overt sexuality are a few of the characteristics we might believe typical of the young woman of the period. Many of these images have been communicated to us through feature films and television documentaries about life in the 1920s, and many of the images used in the latter are clips from *Eve's Film Review*. Of course, only a small proportion of women in the 1920s had the leisure time or financial independence to go dancing all night or to wear clothes at the height of fashion. Women are not a homogeneous whole, and *Eve's Film Review* would have been shown to an audience made up of many types of women; different classes, different ages, and different sexualities, with each woman having a totally different life experience. Pathe, however, made a cinemagazine which they believed would interest *all* women. They offered a screen entertainment that showed women their own likenesses as well as their fantasy selves. Thus films featured women at work in factories and offices as well as female aviators, society girls, and theatrical stars. Ordinary women are featured as well as glamour girls, as the filmmakers attempted to offer women a weekly reflection of womanhood in all its complicated glory.

As these films are rarely seen, a descriptive review of examples from eight main categories forms Chapter 6.

3 – Fashion Fun and Fancy
The Cinemagazine: Format, Thematic Scope and Exhibition Practice

'…a very large proportion of the population, however much they may enjoy a novel, like to be able to entertain themselves with magazines and newspapers. As a parallel, the same people, regular kinema goers though they may be, definitely demand and appreciate the shorter items.'[1]

During the silent period, cinemagoers could expect to see a plethora of short items before settling down for the main feature. In Britain, cinemagazines were a regular part of this experience from 1918, when Pathe released the first issue of the long running weekly *Pathe Pictorial*.[2] Similar to the newsreel in format, the cinemagazine usually ran for around ten minutes, with several separate items within each issue. These items were not linked by theme or story line but were self-contained entities. The unwritten motto of the cinemagazine was 'variety is the spice of life', and items as diverse as fashion parades, animals performing tricks, and demonstrations of household gadgets were contained in the same issue.

The newsreel was seen as being more 'topical' than the cinemagazine. News items were more time-bound than cinemagazine films, turnover was faster, and newsreels were produced twice a week to match the practice of programme changes in the cinema during the silent period. Cinemagazines by contrast were produced weekly. Newsreels had a long life in the silent era, showing for three or four days at each cinema; the reel would circulate for several weeks, with cinema proprietors paying less for the newsreel as it became progressively older. The cinemagazine had an even longer life. Cinemagazine items did not age as swiftly as those of the newsreels; they did not feature subject matter which would date them, such as state occasions or celebrations. The distribution of cinemagazines was a much more leisurely affair. A gentleman who wrote to Pathe in November 1928 asking when he might be able to see an item in which he had appeared, was informed that the *Pathe Pictorial* cinemagazine which contained it would be shown for three days at the following cinemas in his local Bristol area:

Triangle	November 5th, 6th and 7th
Globe	January 25th, 26th and 27th
Vandyke	February 11th, 12th and 13th
North Bath Cinema	February 14th, 15th and 16th

It is very difficult to ascertain how many prints of each cinemagazine were in circulation at any one time. The only clue I have found in the Pathe files is a record of 40 copies of a St Albans colour travel item being ordered from Paris (where the colouring was done) in November 1928. It is possible however that not all of these prints were used in the cinemagazine; some may have been supplied direct to St Albans exhibitors, for example.

Cinema programmes would usually include a combination of newsreel and cinemagazine items. Some cinemas would show reels from a variety of sources. The Piccadilly Cinema in Manchester included the *Gaumont Graphic* newsreel, the *Topical Budget* newsreel, and *Eve's Film Review* in its supporting programme of 1923.[3] Each of these reels was supplied by a different production company.[4] The Thatched Picture House in Norwich had both *Eve's Film Review* and *Pathe Pictorial* on the bill in the mid-1920s,[5] which would have pleased Pathe who promoted the reels thus: 'EVE [is] …a fitting companion to its Monday release partner – the PICTORIAL'.[6] The company offered a discount to exhibitors who took both *Pathe Pictorial* and *Eve's Film Review* and they obviously hoped that cinemas would show *Eve's Film Review* for one half of the week and *Pathe Pictorial* for the other, matching the switch in newsreel issues. As Frederick Watts announced in a press release about his two cinemagazines: 'They are the necessary condiments – the spice of the perfect programme, and we maintain that no programme is complete without them.'[7]

The Spice of the Perfect Programme
It is unlikely that a cinema patron would choose to attend a particular cinema purely on the basis of which cinemagazine was showing. However, film historian Nick Hiley believes that the cinema audience during the silent period often 'bought time in the auditorium rather than access to a particular film'[8], and in this case a good supporting programme might make their visit more enjoyable. As part of an oral history project investigating cinemagoing in the 1930s, Denis Houlston recounted his memories of the 'full supporting programme'. The transcripts of these spoken memories are written in a style to suggest local dialect.

'…looking back at the programmes, there again … you got such a load of little bits, you got a big film but then there were all the little bits and I estimate, lookin back, you used to get about seven different shawrt films to, to boost the programme. So [pause] if you didn't liike any of them you didn't suffer very long because they wouldn't be on for very long!'[9]

18

Although the main feature film would be the biggest drawing factor for cinema patrons at this time, contemporary evidence suggests that other items within the full supporting programme were also enjoyed. In a Sidney Bernstein questionnaire of 1927 it was reported that, 'In reply to the question "Do you like 'News' pictures?", 82¼ per cent of the male patrons voted yes while 87¾ of the female patrons returned the same answer.'[10] That women enjoyed the 'news' pictures even more than men would have been encouraging for the team working on *Eve's Film Review*. The establishment of 'newsreel cinemas' during the mid 1930s, which showed shorts and cinemagazines as well as newsreels, indicates that these peripheral forms of entertainment were indeed enjoyed. Mr Houlston expresses his views on newsreels and cinemagazines as follows:

'Ah mean this is your only way of seeing things happening, the Launching of a Thing, or a crash, or Aa think the Hindenburg went up in flames in those days, Aa might be wrong, and you got the newsreel and that it was really something to see but em nowadays you see it all on television you're blasé so. But Pathé, Pathé news also used to run short films about quarter of an hour or something like that of music-hall acts, a bit of entertainment. You might get a couple in that time and we liked those because you got clowns and eh unicyclists and jugglers which we enjoyed. Aa mean today they wouldn't be of interest. They're all blasé today.'[11]

Topicality Versus Frivolity
'With regard to the criteria used for differentiating between newsreel and cinemagazine, the basic one is that the newsreel carried 'hard news', while the cinemagazine was more like a colour supplement to today's Sunday newspaper.'[12]

Newsreels and cinemagazines aligned themselves with their print predecessors by choosing names that echoed titles of established newspapers and magazines. *Gaumont Graphic*, *Warwick Bioscope Chronicle*, *Pathe Gazette,* and *Topical Budget* were all using terms familiar at the time to describe newspapers (*The Daily Graphic*, *The Daily Chronicle*, *The Pall Mall Gazette,* and *The War Budget* amongst others). Likewise, the cinemagazine *British Screen Tatler* might have been linked in cinemagoers' minds with popular print magazine *The Tatler*. The *Pathe Pictorial* would have been drawing on the strong tradition of magazines such as *Pictorial Mirror*, *Pictorial Review,* and *Lady's Pictorial*.

Just as newspapers and magazines have certain parameters, defining a cinemagazine as different from a newsreel involves making two distinctions; one concerning content, the other concerning style of presentation. The choice of subject matter of the newsreel revolved around notions of what was 'newsworthy', although by virtue of its production and exhibition practices the moving picture news could scarcely match the print newspapers for speediness of reporting. The tardiness of some of its items would have been tolerated for the extra dimension of being able to see the news *move*, and later having sound and moving images together. However, what was considered newsworthy for the moving picture newsreel was not necessarily the same as the news that one would find in a newspaper. As one commentator observed, 'The news obligation is happily trivial. If the newsreels had to cover the news, they would be full of charts on taxes and reports on crop yields. No-one goes to the theatre to get news.'[13] The newsreel was thus limited by the peculiarities of the medium. It could never be just a moving image version of newspaper stories, it had to find its own filmically interesting subjects. Usually these subjects involved movement, the very essence of the 'moving picture' experience. Thus the docking of ships, grand parades and army manoeuvres were the kinds of event favoured by the silent newsreel.

The motto of *Eve's Film Review* was 'Fashion Fun and Fancy', which gives a good idea of the content of cinemagazines in general. The cinemagazine could be seen as being more frivolous than the newsreel, with typical subjects including unusual people, clothes, hobbies, and travel items. The filmmakers of these short entertainments were engaged in 'Searching crazily for the strange and curious'[14] and they offered a glimpse into the many peculiarities of life. Rather than featuring news of national or international importance, the cinemagazine focused on smaller, more intimate things that might today be encompassed by the banner 'lifestyle'. The seemingly frivolous subjects covered by the cinemagazine can tell us much about the daily lives of ordinary people of the past.

As an illustration of the difference in typical content of newsreels and cinemagazines, there follows a breakdown of items in an issue of *Eve's Film Review*, compared with an issue of *British Movietone News*, both released in late 1932.

Eve's Film Review issue 596
Release date 3rd November 1932

British Movietone News issue 177A
Release date 27th October 1932

To Pluck or Not to Pluck [eyebrows]
A Marriage has been Arranged [in Korea]
Happy Schooldays [French kindergarten]
Leaps & Bounds [Lacrosse]

British Ocean Giants Dock Together
Hitler Visits Scene of Royal Wedding
Fatal Rail Crash Occurs in France
Britain is to Stage World Title Fight
Mussolini Reviews his Policemen
U.S. Commentator Guys Kid Yachtsman

Whilst the focus of the newsreel is upon political leaders, traditionally male sports (boxing and competitive sailing) and a recent disaster in France, the cinemagazine features feminine beauty, marriage, children and a traditionally female sport. The 'gendering' of content in these non-narrative films is something that involves many complex assumptions about what film-makers thought would be of interest to different genders, and beyond this whether there was a fundamental difference between the male and female spectator. I will explore these issues later in this study, but it seems to me that *in general* the newsreel addressed a male audience and the cinemagazine a female audience.

The subject matter of the newsreel was usually proposed as being 'serious'. A respectful, sombre, impartial tone of reporting was called for, and was achieved through titles in silent newsreels and through tone of voice in sound reels. Within the cinemagazine the style of reporting is much less deferential and more often than not commentaries were jokey and intimate. An intertitle in a *Topical Budget* newsreel item covering the funeral of Queen Alexandra in November 1925 illustrates the general tone of address of the newsreel: 'In London the people crowned her death with their grief and the heavens sent her a white shroud.'[15] By comparison, an *Eve's Film Review* item instructing women how to apply false eyelashes has an intertitle typical of the cinemagazines' witty banter: 'Her eyes swept the floor – They could have swept a park had they been aided by this latest beauty fad'.[16]

Although only *Eve's Film Review* was promoted specifically as a weekly women's film, other cinemagazines also contained much more subject matter traditionally thought of as 'feminine interest' than did the newsreel. *The Gaumont Mirror* cinemagazine for example featured fashion, beauty and female sport alongside less gender-specific items. Thus while the newsreel was largely seen as an information source for male cinemagoers, it is fair to assume that the cinemagazine was addressing itself directly to the female audience.

The 'Musical Dog' of the Newsreel
The distinction between the content (and tone of address) of cinemagazines and that of newsreels was not always clear-cut. Both formats did stray across the boundaries from time to time, the newsreel more so than the cinemagazine. The supposedly solemn newsreel often carried items which were not time-specific and which contrasted in tone with the seriousness of other items, with titles such as *Musical Dog*, *Wrestling with a Lion* and *Patterns made in the water by 64 German ladies*.[17]

It could be that sometimes the subjects that usually fell into the loose newsreel category of 'real news' were scarce, or it could be that the production company felt that a less serious item would 'lighten' the tone. Peter Baechlin and Maurice

Muller-Strauss published a survey of newsreels around the world in 1952. Although their findings relate to a much later period than that under consideration here, they throw light on the mixing of subject matter in the newsreels. They propose three main categories for newsreel subjects: sudden events of immediate interest; scheduled events; and items of a general interest not necessarily connected with topical affairs. The latter items were those 'dealing with local customs and traditions, pictures of bathing beauties and "pin-up girls", religious or traditional festivals … in short, all those items which editors keep in reserve for the "dull" weeks when there is a shortage of items of the first and second categories.'[18] Thus a *Topical Budget* newsreel which featured the launch of the H.M.S. Nelson and the destruction of the Shenandoah could also feature 'Amesbury's prettiest girl, Miss Margery Waller' and 'the dog show at Brighton.'[19] It is interesting to note that the items of general interest listed by Baechlin and Muller-Strauss are a fairly accurate guide to the type of subject favoured by the cinemagazine.

The tradition of ending a television news bulletin with a jokey or happy story was foreshadowed by cinema newsreels, as this review of *Gaumont Graphic* issue number 1,815 illustrates: 'The Prince of Wales and 11,000 British pilgrims pay silent homage to our dead at the Menin Gate ceremony at Ypres, and we are shown the impressive two-minute silence which marked the solemn occasion … A huge fire of six great oil tanks on Wood River, Illinois, and jockeys on the Spree, a diversion on Berlin's river, which brings the issue to an amusing conclusion.'[20] Some critics disagreed with this mixing of tones, and one contemporary writer expressed his views thus: 'There should, of course, be a mutual understanding that both types of film must remember their respective places, for this broadening of the field of the newsreel is tending to undermine the interest film.'[21] The cinemagazine was rather more constant in avoiding the serious topics and tone favoured by the newsreel; however we cannot dismiss the form as consisting entirely of 'Fashion Fun and Fancy'.

A Serious Side to the Cinemagazine?
The editor of *Pathe Pictorial* and *Eve's Film Review* wrote in a press release in 1928:

'We realise our primary business is to entertain, amuse and interest our audiences – though, if at the same time anyone wishes to learn anything new from the pictures (and all of us are able to) he or she is very welcome.'[22]

This statement underlines the tension at the heart of the cinemagazine. On the one hand it had to have the potential to entertain, otherwise the cinema owner would not hire it. On the other hand, many felt that it should educate and inform its audiences at the same time. A comparison with the aims and achievements of

22

the British documentary is revealing. This movement is popularly believed to have begun in the late 1920s with the John Grierson school. It is worth remembering, however, that the cinemagazine had been a forum for short, informative films of everyday life since the late 1910s.[23]

Pathe Pictorial had two mottoes in the 1920s. These were: '*Pathe Pictorial* Puts the World Before You' and 'To See Much is to Learn Much'. Such sentiments were typical of the cinemagazine and its efforts to show audiences the wonders of the world around them. Since it existed outside the exigencies of narrative justification, it was in a unique position whereby almost anything could be shown and one does get the feeling that 'all human life is here'. The cinemagazine also reached far wider audiences than any of the documentaries made by Grierson and his colleagues.

Writing in 1932, Andrew Buchanan, producer of the *Ideal Cinemagazine*, uses terms that quite explicitly bring to mind the concerns of the 1930s documentarists:

'The fact that the interest reel is non-fictional is its greatest advantage over the dramatic feature. It can bring to the screen places near and far, industries, sports, clothes, everything which constitutes Life, without straining to find a reason for doing so.'[24]

For some commentators however, the cinemagazine failed to make the most of its didactic and edificatory potential. Criticisms were made of the cinemagazine that it did not tackle 'serious issues' such as social problems, slums, and unemployment. Writing in *Cinema Quarterly*, a magazine with close links to the documentary movement, D.F. Taylor launched an assault on the cinemagazine for its insistence on 'a low form of entertainment', characterised by 'a dash of industry, a dash of beauteous countryside, two dashes of fashion and a lacing of cabaret to give the reel a kick'. He writes:

'Far from seeking an opiate, there is a large body of people who want to know more about this crazy, chaotic world … Through the screen magazine, the thin end of the wedge of knowledge could be given to the waiting audiences … [However] Its constant seeking after the odd and the curious satisfies the unintelligent lust for curiosity but achieves nothing.'[25]

With grand plans for 'improving' the cinemagazine to 'improve' the audience he suggests that the producers of cinemagazines should place a greater emphasis on education and information:

'through the magazine, we have an aid to socially conscious cinema. It has a journalistic format, and as such it is of value. We want to elevate it from the ranks of *"Tit-Bits"*; we want to make it a weekly review of the world.'[26]

What is evident in Taylor's argument is a familiar suspicion of both popular culture and feminine culture. While the cinemagazine might not have dealt with such issues as social problems, slums, and unemployment, this did not mean it was divorced from the process of educating and informing. For example, within *Eve's Film Review* there are many items which document the reality of women's lives with a didactic seriousness – (see Chapter 6). Many of the items showing women at work eschew the usual humorous titles and merely illustrate the tasks performed. *Tennis Trifles* for example shows women in a factory making tennis balls and each procedure is explained step by step. *Light On Turkish Delight* shows women working in a sweet factory. Home sewing tips are given in *Odds and Ends* as a mother makes a pinafore for her daughter. Techniques for making things for the home are demonstrated in *Sealing-wax Stunts* and timesaving devices are demonstrated in *Gadgets for Eve*. The idea that the cinemagazine offers a 'window on the world' is also apparent in *Eve's Film Review*, with items about women in foreign lands, such as: *The Canoe Girls of Ngaruawahia*, *The Bride of the Black Forest*, and *Fisher Girls of Ostend*. As an accompaniment to the feature, which often portrayed a fantasy life out of reach for most of the cinema audience, the cinemagazine could offer a slice of comparative reality and could educate and enlighten as well as entertain.

Men's Pleasures = Serious, Women's Pleasures = Frivolous?

Discussions about the frivolous and the serious involve certain value judgments about the 'usefulness' and 'merit' of *Eve's Film Review*. Although I want to show that there was a space within this cinemagazine for illuminating films showing women's everyday experience, I do not propose that these items are of more 'worth' than the more numerous 'Fashion Fun and Fancy' items. The informative films sit alongside the less 'serious' items and complement them. It is true, however, that most of the items in *Eve's Film Review* are of a somewhat frivolous nature.

Women's pleasures have been trivialised throughout history and by choosing to make a cinemagazine for women (rather than a newsreel for women) Pathe were working within a form which was seen by many as desultory and lightweight. The editor of *Eve's Film Review* himself described it as 'a most comprehensive and attractive "light" periodical.'[27] A format which focused on issues such as fashion, feminine beauty, home-making and marriage rather than wars, disasters, and politics could be criticised from the position of seeing women's pleasures as being less important than male pleasures. This position, however, is gradually being unsteadied by studies focusing on areas such as the romance novel and women's print magazines. Recent forays into the field of 'popular entertainment' have reclaimed forms hitherto labelled as trashy; the musical, the melodrama and music hall comedy are now seen as having historical and cultural significance. There can be no doubt that the seemingly frivolous items within *Eve's Film Review* are more than worthy of study.

Cinemagazines and the 'Cinema of Attractions'

The cinemagazine has a strong relationship with the earlier modes of filmic representation identified by Tom Gunning as the 'cinema of attractions'.[28] His findings are important when we look at the cinemagazine as a screened entertainment that existed outside the conventions of the narrative film. Gunning offers a way of approaching early film which does not see it as being merely the forerunner of a purer, more systematic mode of representation which emerged with the dominance of the narrative film and continuity editing. He draws attention to elements within early film representation that are *not* precursors to what has come to be known as 'classical cinema'. He also claims that with the burgeoning dominance of narrative that began around 1906-7, the 'cinema of attractions' was forced to go 'underground' into certain avant-garde practices and as a component of narrative films such as the musical. It is my contention however, that elements of 'the cinema of attractions' remained highly visible within the 'full supporting programme' and in particular within the cinemagazine.

This idea is relevant to a study of *Eve's Film Review* as it provides a framework in which to place the cinemagazine as an entity which accompanied the feature film, but in many ways was very different from it. I will therefore describe certain features of what Gunning calls 'the cinema of attractions' and illustrate how I believe they survive within *Eve's Film Review*.

Showing Rather Than Telling

Cinemagazine items are firmly based on the cinema of attractions' predilection for showing rather than telling. This is a non-narrative form where rather than being told a story, we are shown something: a scenic view, the latest fashion in footwear, or a four year old child driving a car in the streets of Paris. These items are presented as glimpses of the many facets of human experience.

The cinemagazine fashion item illustrates very well Gunning's notion of the supply of pleasure through spectacle which characterises the cinema of attractions. It is ostensibly the clothes which are being shown to the audience in these short fashion parades, although the women who model the clothes are themselves on display. Films such as *Costumes for Sea and See* offer the chance to enjoy seeing women lounging around modelling swim-wear, turning slowly and seductively so that we can appreciate their figures as much as their outfits:

25

(5) Clothes on Display – Costumes for Sea and See

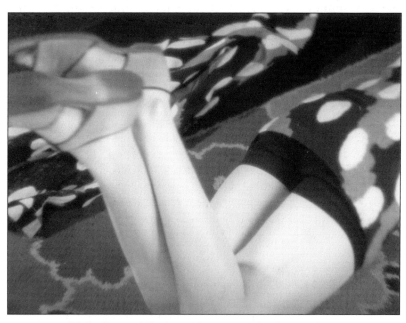

(6) Bodies on Display – Costumes for Sea and See

5 and 6. An intertitle invites us to enjoy 'The bathing suit of the Season (including contents)'. Other items which do not centre on clothes also feature elements of spectacle. Many *Eve's Film Review* items featuring sportswomen focus on the beauty of movement, often filming sporting achievements in slow motion. An intertitle in *More Half and Half Pictures* preceding shots of a woman diving into a pool and swimming underwater reads: 'And the slow-motion camera makes sure that nothing of this perfect Miss is missed.'

Direct Address to the Audience

Within the cinema of attractions Gunning also identifies a particular relationship to the audience which differs from that of the classical mode of representation. This is typified by 'the recurring look at the camera by actors'.[29] Gunning observes that this look became taboo within the dominant mode of representation, only occurring now and again in moments of excess in the musical or in comic asides to camera. But the look at the camera is also a feature of the cinemagazine and newsreel. Although in the newsreel the look is usually naive (a person who notices the camera for example), within the cinemagazine it is more often a 'knowing' look, an exhibitionist look. It is an address to the spectator which says, 'look at me – I am showing you something'. Within *Eve's Film Review* these looks occur in abundance, especially among the fashion display items. In an item entitled *Hair Fashions* for example, a woman poses with a feather fan, looking seductively at the camera and by implication at the audience: 7. In some of the fashion items models wink at the camera. As Gunning observes, the acknowledgement of the spectator as voyeur by this form of direct address can often give these moving images an intense erotic power.[30] The proliferation of looks to camera within *Eve's Film Review* will be explored further in a later chapter of this book.

The Cinematic Apparatus Itself as an Attraction

Gunning notes how in the early days of cinema, the machinery of cinema was in itself an attraction. Audiences would come to see developments in technology rather than to view specific films. It seems to me that the cinemagazine provided a forum outside of the main feature film where experiments with the medium could continue to take place. Of *Pathe Pictorial* and *Pathetone Weekly* (*Eve's Film Review* had ceased production at the time this was written but could be included as a stable-mate) an uncredited author writes:

'Every camera development and novelty may be said at one time or other to have originated in various forms through the medium of these weeklies. The cartoon vogue, slow motion, stop motion, colour sections, reverse photography, multiple exposure novelties, sporting series, fashion and all forms of industrial and scientific progress have been featured.'[31]

(7) Direct address to the camera – Hair Fashions

(8) Camera tricks – Fresh Air Frolics

Although one would now challenge the idea that some of these innovations actually originated within the cinemagazine (recalling the trick photography of Georges Méliès for example), it is true to say that they continued to be used in the cinemagazine rather than disappearing from the screen altogether. *Eve's Film Review* items such as *The Lens Liar – (The Camera Cannot Lie…?)* made explicit the possibilities of the cinematic medium with reverse motion and fast motion footage of swimming and diving. *Fresh Air Frolics* used optical printing to superimpose women dancers over shots of a cloudy sky: **8** and *The Keep Fit Brigade* had shots of dancing women superimposed on a man's outstretched arm: **9**. Slow motion photography was used in many dance, sport and 'girls at play' items.

The cinemagazine could be thought of as the research and development section of the film industry. With no narrative restrictions or diegetic effect to maintain, such self-conscious devices were totally acceptable and the cinemagazine became the site of playful experimentation.

(9) Camera Tricks – The Keep Fit Brigade

The Concept of Variety – a Series of Discrete Attractions

The early, short films that Gunning speaks of in terms of the cinema of attractions found their niche within the variety programmes of vaudeville, music hall and fairgrounds, in which a trick film may have been shown between a farce and an actuality. The cinemagazine too was sandwiched between other items on the cinema programme including live variety acts, newsreels, cartoons, serials, short features and the main feature. The cinemagazine is thus one attraction of the many attractions within the cinemagoing experience of the late 1910s onwards.

There is also variety within the cinemagazine itself. In fact, variety could be thought of as the *modus operandi* of the cinemagazine. **10** shows an advertisement for an *Eve's Film Review* release with a varied selection of subject matter and cinematic forms.[32] Unconnected items are shown side by side without any attempt to link them together and can be understood without reference to their neighbours.

Cinemagazines of Attractions

The cinemagazine was a form within which elements of the cinema of attractions survived and flourished. It could deal with a much wider range of subject matter and use more experimental techniques than the narrative-bound film with its striving for 'realism'. The form seemed to scoop up all those bits and pieces that early film-makers relished but which had been gradually pushed to the edges of the main feature: travel items, semi-pornographic displays of the female body, music hall acts, and so on. Although these aspects were often made a part of feature films of the time, the narrative might strain to incorporate them. In the cinemagazine, these attractions were there to entertain and sometimes to inform without any justification or attempts to weave the spectacle into a narrative. Using techniques which had disappeared from the narrative film, the cinemagazine often brought film-making processes to the fore. This resulted in an interactive relationship with the audience.

The Longevity of the Form

Pathe produced the *Pathe Pictorial* weekly from 1918 until 1969, its long life surely proof that the cinemagazine was valued by many exhibitors and cinemagoers. *Eve's Film Review* ceased production in 1933, twelve years after it was launched. There are many possible reasons for the end of the cinemagazine for women, the largest of which was probably economic. By 1930 Pathe was producing a twice weekly newsreel and three cinemagazines. Frederick Watts had added a new sound cinemagazine called *Pathetone Weekly* to his output. As the number of cinemas declined during the early 1930s and more of them became equipped for sound, it is quite likely that the company decided to consolidate its cinemagazine productions to concentrate on the two sound reels (*Pathe Pictorial* became the

EVE – AND EVERYBODY'S
FILM REVIEW

FASHION, STAGE, HOME, SPORT, Etc., Etc.

CONTENTS OF No. 143.

(1) MISS CANADA IN WINTERTIME.

In Canada the low temperature does not affect Eve's high spirits. We found her game for any sport in the snow, and given a toboggan—and an Adam or two—she can make any country fit for Zeros.

(2) COMBS FOR EVE.

At first glance it is difficult to credit the rough tortoise with such a fine shell for "combing out." The first operation is selecting the best pieces and marking and cutting out the patterns, after which the rough surface has to be scraped and sand-papered. The comb then has a bath in hot brine to soften the shell, which is then bent to the shape required, and is finally polished.

(3) MIXING IT.

Did you ever have a day go wrong—get all mixed up so to speak? In this picture we are going to show you some more of our wonderful "lens liar" series.

(4) THE LONG AND THE SHORT OF IT. (Pathécolor.)

Once more the hardy old struggle between longer or shorter skirts has recommenced, and in these latest creations Paris displays both.

(5) ADVENTURES OF FELIX THE CAT. (Cartoon.)

PATHÉ FRÈRES CINEMA, LTD.
84, WARDOUR STREET, LONDON, W.1

Branches :

LEEDS, 1-8, Wellington Chambers	BIRMINGHAM, 303, Broad Street
LIVERPOOL, 34, Paradise Street	CARDIFF 13, Charles Street
MANCHESTER, 15, Deansgate	DUBLIN, 2, Lower Abbey Street
NEWCASTLE 208, Westgate Road	GLASGOW, 80, Mille Street

(10) Variety bill – Eve's Film Review *publicity handout*

Pathe Sound Pictorial in 1931).[33] However, the subjects which Pathe considered to be of particular interest to women did not disappear from the screen altogether with the death of *Eve's Film Review*. Fashion and beauty tips, women's sports and pastimes all featured in the *Pathe Sound Pictorial* and *Pathetone Weekly* alongside less gender-specific and more masculine subjects. An item called *For Thee Alone Madame (But Gentlemen May Glance)* in a *Pathetone Weekly* of 1934 illustrates that Pathe continued to suggest that men would be interested in women's fashion items. The sobriquet of 'Eve' as designator of the fair sex lived on too in stories such as *From Eve to Everywoman* in a *Pathetone Weekly* of 1936, but never again would there be a weekly cinema presentation so full of fashion, fun and fancy, and specifically made for women.

4 – Powder Puff Culture
Femininity, the New Woman and Eve in the 1920s and Early 1930s

'... with short hair, skirts a little longer than kilts, narrow hips, insignificant breasts, there has arrived a confident, active, game-loving capable human being, who shuns the servitude of household occupations. With her smaller, lither, more ornamental figure and greater capabilities, she has ousted the less capable or less fortunate men out of their occupations ... this change to a more neutral type ... can be accomplished only at the expense of the integrity of her sexual organs.'[1]

In Britain during the 1920s there was an unprecedented interest in what was seen to be a new visibility of female sexuality, and in the gradual infiltration of traditionally male spheres by women. This interest was a reaction to many changes that had taken place in women's lives during the First World War and was also a response to the struggle for universal suffrage that was taking place at this time. Many contemporary commentators expressed the view that 'femininity' was under threat from the mannish dress and behaviour of some 'modern women'. Shared perceptions, prejudices and ideas about 'the new woman' were circulated in newspapers and magazines and through the cinema, many of them critical of new freedoms available at this time. In this overview of contemporary opinions towards women I hope to provide some historical context for the debates and themes running through *Eve's Film Review.*

The Rival Sex
'In the eyes of many contemporaries, a society in which fertile females were plentiful and males were scarce was politically, socially and morally imperilled.'[2]

In the years following the First World War there was a considerable demographic imbalance in Britain – the death of a generation of men had left almost two million women without partners. In the press of the time this was a subject much discussed and although at first this imbalance was referred to as a 'surplus of women', the catch phrase was modified slightly to become the more detrimental 'superfluous women'. This household phrase (which may have been coined by Viscount Northcliffe, the owner of the *Daily Mail*, in 1921) reverberated throughout the 1920s and early 1930s and implied that a woman who was without a partner and who did not produce children was of no use to society. Clemence Dane described these women in 1929 as: 'Spinsters of this great parish … the band of nearly 2,000,000 women who will always remain single, loveless, childless.'[3] However, a considerable drop in the birth rate after the First World War was probably a result of the gradual legitimisation of contraceptives as well as the lack of male partners, so it could be inferred that for some women the childless state was one of choice.

The debate around the 'problem' of two million women of reproductive age without husbands and children became centred on two fluctuating and overlapping ideas of the 'modern woman'. Firstly 'the flapper', a young woman of independent means who flaunted her sexuality, and secondly (less class and age specific), the woman who had begun to make herself known in traditionally male domains: the workplace, the sports field and the political arena. Although these two problematic women seem at first to be very different, they share the position of being women who are becoming 'more like men'. Sexual and social boundaries are blurred and the male notion of supremacy is threatened.

The term 'flapper' had many different meanings during the 1921-1933 period under discussion here. It was not used simply to define certain styles of dress and behaviour as it has come to do in the twenty-first century. Billie Melman has traced the origins of the term 'flapper' in her excellent book *Women and the Popular Imagination in the Twenties – Flappers and Nymphs*. Originally used to describe a young bird just able to fly, the term came to signify a female adolescent on the eve of her debut in society around 1870. At this time the word had also come to signify a child prostitute in some circles and this link between innocence and sexuality continued to be an underlying aspect of the term as it grew in usage. The term took on a specific political meaning just after the First World War in that it began to describe a disenfranchised young woman: 'Flapper is the catchword for an adult woman aged 21-30 when it is a question of giving her the vote under the same qualification as men of the same age.'[4] The campaign for universal suffrage found its main objection in the fact that if the 'flapper vote' were granted, women would outnumber men on the electoral roll with 14½ million women compared with 12¼ million men.[5] Many owners of newspapers were avowedly against universal suffrage and this may be one reason why the perpetuation of the myth of the silly, frivolous woman was given space in their papers. The *Daily Mail* for example warned of the: 'risks from the voting of impulsive and politically ignorant girls' whose votes were likely to reflect the 'foolish Communistic sentiments of their boyfriends.'[6]

The dangers of the 'flapper vote' became the focus of many debates about women entering traditionally male domains and threatening the status quo. Helena Normanton (who became the first woman barrister in Britain in 1921) wrote in 1926:

'Men do not want women in politics. Neither do they at the Bar, nor the Stock Exchange, nor on the Episcopal Bench, nor in the priesthood, nor in fact in any seats of authority. It means for men, too much adjustment for themselves. The old ways have suited them very nicely all down the centuries.'[7]

Many 'superfluous' women had taken work during the war and continued to do so in the period following it (although working class women had long been in employment, this period saw an increase in female employment in all classes). This precipitated a general rise in the standard of living for women and a subsequent growth in their spending power. There was a great deal of resistance to the fact that women were moving away from the home and into the workplace. Working women were criticised if it was thought that they were taking a job that should be given to a man. Once the war was over, married women were actively discouraged from working and some took to removing their wedding rings and calling themselves 'Miss' rather than 'Mrs'. As Irene Clephane observed:

'From being the saviours of the nation, women in employment were degraded in the … press to the position of ruthless self-seekers depriving men and their dependents of a livelihood … all of them became, in many people's minds, objects of opprobrium.'[8]

The Modern Woman

Every age has its own ideas about what constitutes the 'new' or 'modern' woman so that attitudes, roles and occupations are in a constant state of flux. In the 1920s ideas of what made a woman 'modern' were grouped around two main factors: her eagerness to be 'one of the boys' and an open attitude to her own sexuality. That some saw both these attributes as frightening can be seen in magazines and newspapers of the time and within *Eve's Film Review*. In the popular press, the disenfranchised young woman was endowed with distinct characteristics revolving around the expression of sexuality through dress and behaviour. The fact that fashions were becoming more androgynous was perhaps related to the struggle to gain the vote; however this could also be seen as an indication that for a woman to be considered 'modern' in any era she has to imitate men.

The acquisition of 'unfeminine' or 'masculine' characteristics of dress, figure and attitudes to sport and work was often depicted as unnatural and freakish. The striving after the boyish figure so fashionable at this time was seen as potentially dangerous to women's sexual reproductive systems, as was participation in vigorous sports. This view is illustrated in *Eve's Film Review* intertitles such as 'Certain Medical quarters are beginning to consider seriously whether Eve, in her new-found freedom is not taking up athletics too strenuously'.[9] There is much discussion within *Eve's Film Review* items of how far the 'woman of today' has come with comparisons to the fashions and codes of conduct of earlier years. Smoking was often seen as a 'modern' habit and several films show the horror with which this practice might be seen by women of the past: **11**. The propensity to show increasingly more flesh is often remarked upon in swim-wear items such as *Eve in the Swim* ('With the passing years, one sees more and more of Eve') and items such as *The Beach Censor* where a tape measure is used to check that swimsuits are an appropriate length: **12**. That women's sexuality was often seen as potentially threatening is amusingly illustrated in *The Buffer Belt – a Paris Novelty*. This was a device to prevent men and women from touching nether regions whilst dancing: **13**.[10]

Both stereotypes of women in the 1920s – the sexually liberated flapper, and the mannish woman who could hold her own in the man's world – were seen as a threat because they denied men offspring in favour of living a full and exciting life. I am not suggesting here that motherhood prevents women from leading full and exciting lives, but rather in the 1920s women who chose not to have children were often depicted as selfish, freakish and unfeminine. A 1929 article entitled *Our Super Women* is full of praise for flappers who 'earn their own livelihood', lead 'a hectic life' and 'can stay the course, not only at play but at work too'. However, the gender of the author and his anxiety about the flapper's sexuality are revealed at the very end of the piece:

'Poor man! Unequal partner of this Super-Being. No wonder he applauds any disparagement of the new super-woman. His carefully erected pedestal has been undermined, the secret places of his business unveiled, authority snatched from him. And now his last monopoly is gone; for super-women sow wild oats and reap not where they sow.'[11]

The Sex Novel and the Flapper
However, while male journalists expressed their anxieties through the popular newspapers, women writers began to celebrate the new freedoms and possibilities available to their contemporaries. The post war period saw a blossoming of women's periodicals and escapist forms of fiction. Many magazine articles were penned by women and the new phenomenon of the 'best seller' was spearheaded by writers such as Margaret Kennedy with *The Constant Nymph* (1924), and Elinor Glyn with *It* (1927) and *The Flirt and the Flapper* (1922). For women writers of literature and film scenarios, the persona of the flapper

(11)
The smoking habit –
Understandings

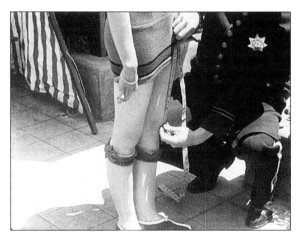

(12)
Inch by inch –
The Beach Censor

(13)
Keep back! –
The Buffer Belt –
a Paris Novelty

provided an ideal forum for discussion and dramatisation of female sexuality. One type of narrative was singled out at the time and labelled 'the sex novel'. Billie Melman describes it thus:

'First and foremost, the heroine was a contemporary young woman. Second the genre displayed an obsession with modern sexual morality. Third, it provided a realistic presentation of women's sexual experience and openly discussed the topic of female sexuality.'[12]

One of the most successful 'sex novels' of the period, Elinor Glyn's *It* was made into a Hollywood movie in 1927. It featured the quintessential screen flapper Clara Bow – thenceforth known as 'The "It" Girl' (the word 'It' being a euphemism for a certain sexual attraction). Clara was the flapper personified and a feature in *Motion Picture Classic* of March 1927 describes 'The equipment of Clara Bow's toggery'. The male writer expresses mock horror at the cost and intricacies of a flapper's wardrobe.

Clothes, accessories and make-up were the major trappings of the flapper persona within the cinema and the popular press. Male journalists attempted to keep up with the vagaries of fashion, with skirt lengths being of particular interest. Their yo-yoing throughout the 1920s and early 1930s was also often commented upon in *Eve's Film Review*. In the film *Paris Fashions in Advance* an intertitle observes: 'Joseph Paquin again helps the optical industry by shortening the skirts' and in *Understandings* another reads: 'Skirts started near the ground – but goodness knows where they'll finish!'. Alternations between ultra feminine (diaphanous fabrics, fringes and beads for example) and androgynous looks often provided cartoonists and commentators with material for satirical comment. An *Eve's Film Review* item entitled *Dresses and Tresses* features a woman dressed in a man's suit and another in a frilly frock. An intertitle reads: 'Comment is useless. Their dresses are entirely out of harmony with their hair'. The girl in the floaty frock has a very severe bob haircut whilst the woman in the more mannish clothes has a longer, more fluffy do. This offers the Pathe cameraman the opportunity to film the girls swapping clothes so that the short haired girl can wear the suit and look mannish smoking a cigarette with her hand in her pocket and the other can be feminine and girly. Several films played with the idea of androgyny, with an outstanding example being *Pyjama Peeps* where a model wears batik pyjamas and poses hand on hip and legs akimbo as she smokes: **14**. She is seen earlier admiring another woman's outfit and the interaction between the two carries connotations that they are more than just good friends.

Print magazines of the time positively revelled in the kaleidoscopic ever-changing image of 'the modern woman' and their pages are full of fashion spreads celebrating the latest novelties of dress. The woman's magazine offered

(14) Smoking pyjamas – Pyjama Peeps

a forum for discussion of the elusive and ever changing concept of femininity. As Margaret Beetham observes, these periodicals served as advisors to women on the many and various expressions of womanhood. The following description could also be applied to *Eve's Film Review* as well as to the print magazine:

'The assumption of femininity as simultaneously natural and culturally acquired through labour sets up a complex tension for the reader. On the one hand she is addressed as already 'woman' – this is, after all, the ground on which she is identified as a reader. On the other hand, there is a clear gap between what she is, and what the magazines claims she "ought" (to desire) to be. Femininity, therefore, becomes both a source of anxiety and a source of pleasure because it can never be fully achieved. The magazines perpetuate this myth of femininity and offer themselves as a solution. The magazine will be friend, advisor and instructor in the difficult task of being a woman.'[13]

As well as articles on the trappings of femininity, new freedoms and opportunities for women are celebrated within contemporary magazines as women entered domains previously considered purely for the boys. Articles are written *by* women *for* women. A magazine of particular interest to a discussion of *Eve's Film Review* is *Eve the Lady's Pictorial* which was on the market at the same time as the cinemagazine and shared many of the same characteristics.

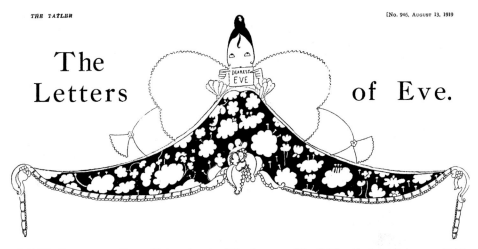

The Letters of Eve.

(16) The Eponymous Eve – illustration for "The Letters of Eve", The Tatler 13 August 1919

Eve the Lady's Pictorial

Two years before the first issue of *Eve's Film Review* hit the screens, a print magazine bearing the title *Eve* had hit the newsstands. This monthly magazine was extremely popular and soon became a weekly, merging with the *Lady's Pictorial* in 1921 to become the more evocative *Eve the Lady's Pictorial*: **15**. The launch of the new magazine had probably been prompted by the very popular column 'The Letters of Eve' which ran in the *The Tatler* from 1914 to 1920.[14] This column had an eponymous author who commented on subjects such as women authors, the institution of marriage, food shortages, and art exhibitions. The prose was written in a chatty, familiar style as if from one friend to another, for example:

'My Dear Betty – S'nice in the country, isn't it, now there isn't any more war? But demoralisin'. F'rinstance – in town – well, you know my well-known energy, don't you? But here in Arcadia I simply don't want to do nothing – not even write to you, Best Beloved.'[15]

The column featured cute line drawings of Eve by the respected female cartoonist 'Fish': **16** and was the inspiration for three books and a 12 part film series called *The Adventures of Eve*: **17**.[16] The films starred actress Eileen Molyneux and were presumably in the style of other serials of the day with eponymous heroines, such as *The Exploits of Elaine* and *The Perils of Pauline*. Alas, none of the *Adventures of Eve* films are known to survive but from the evidence of episode titles, Eve's adventures were somewhat more tame than her American contemporaries. Instalments included: *Eve Adopts a Lonely Soldier*, *Eve and the Nervous Curate* and *Eve Goes to the East Coast*.

(15)
"Home Jane!" –
Cover for
Eve The Lady's
Pictorial

(17)
Eve gets her own film series –
The Adventures of Eve –
advertisement in
The Kinematograph and
Lantern Weekly
25 July 1918

The new weekly print magazine *Eve the Lady's Pictorial* was a glossy production covering topics such as society gossip, fashion, beauty, sport, motoring, pets, and housekeeping. Priced at one shilling the magazine was affordable and appealing, full of glorious illustrations and witty columns.[17] A few men wrote for women's magazines under their own names at this time but most articles within *Eve the Lady's Pictorial* were presented as if written by women, often in an epistolary format with a chatty tone.[18] Some of the articles bearing a woman's signature may well have been written by men under pseudonyms. The writing style and terms of address however, are of a style which has come to be defined as 'feminine' i.e. chatty, informal, friendly and implying a common understanding of desires and problems seen as being specific to women. The concept of 'Eve' as being the author of the entire magazine and a friend and confidante of the reader is expressed in the introductory editorial of the first issue:

'The first love, the first voyage, the first achievement – any of our first experiences are milestones which punctuate our passage along the winding road of Life. It is the sincere wish of "EVE" that this, her first number, should prove to be a milestone marking the foundation of a long and lasting friendship between you, fair reader, and herself.'[19]

That the editor strikes the pose of 'Eve' even though he is probably a man (most likely Edward Huskinson) marks an interesting cross-gender writing style which runs throughout the magazine.[20]

Although many things mark the implied reader of *Eve the Lady's Pictorial* as upper-class (society gossip) and educated (the use of the French language without English translation), the magazine probably had a much broader readership. Ros Ballaster writes: 'Publishers and editors recognise their readers as "aspirational", aspiring to be older (in the case of teenagers), richer, thinner, in a higher class or social bracket.'[21] This idea of the aspirational reader can also be applied to *Eve's Film Review,* since many of the fashion items feature haute couture clothes which would surely have been out of reach for many of the cinemagazine's spectators.

The fact that there had been many changes in the lives of women since the First World War is a recurring theme of interest in both print magazines of the time and in *Eve's Film Review*. The pre-publication advertisement for the print magazine *Eve* proclaimed it to be 'The New Weekly for The New Woman' and defined its potential readership as 'the woman of to-day whose whole outlook and interests have been immeasurably enlarged by the events of the past five years': **18**. However, these changes are discussed only in terms of social and not political differences. Comments about changes in the political sphere are conspicuous by their absence both from most women's magazines of the period

The New Weekly

for

The New Woman

Eve is a high-class Woman's paper—the woman of to-day whose whole outlook and interests have been immeasureably enlarged by the events of the past five years.

Eve is clean, healthy, bright, and above all, " English ! "

Eve is an Illustrated Weekly survey of every person and every subject and thing that the educated woman of to-day is talking about. It will find a welcome in all cultured Homes, and therefore cannot fail to prove an excellent medium for advertisers who appeal to the educated Women of England.

(18)
The New Weekly for The New Woman – advertisement for Eve
in the Newspaper Press Directory 1921

and from *Eve's Film Review*. Although many women were fighting for universal suffrage it seems that politics was not thought to be a suitable subject for these forums unless in a jokey way through asides in intertitles in the film magazine, and through advertising in the print magazine. For example, Abdulla cigarettes were advertised in 1929 with a drawing of a quintessential flapper in cloche hat and short skirt smoking with her hand on her hip. A little rhyme by F.R. Holmes underneath the drawing concludes as follows:

"Male M.P.'s are no longer in fashion", states Claudia, enchantingly grim.
"You must vote for high-soul-powered Women, alert and volcanic with vim.
"Friends and Flappers," smiles Claudia the cunning, "if you care to elect
  little Me,
"The State shall supply your silk stockings, and every Abdulla be free."[22]

The main interest of *Eve the Lady's Pictorial* is fashion not politics, and like *Eve's Film Review* it looks towards Paris for the latest chic styles. A weekly three page article called 'Eve in Paris/Paradise' details the exploits of a young, fashionable lady of leisure and is announced as 'A little parable of the eternal feminine, which indicates as it unwinds the tendencies of the fashions which are today intriguing the hearts and minds of "the sex" in the Gay City.'[23] Eve lives with a man; whether he is her husband or lover we are never explicitly informed. Her relationship with him sets the tone for the magazine's attitude to men in general (an occasional cookery column is called, 'Feed the Brute' for example). She calls him 'That awful Adam!' and criticises him for weaknesses she infers are typical of the male sex,

(19)
Do you like
what you see? –
Eve December 1919

such as jealousy (when she dances with other men) and his tendency to drink too much. That Adam and Eve have an exciting sexual relationship is hinted at within the text, and the drawings which accompany it: **19**.

Unfortunately no distribution figures exist for *Eve the Lady's Pictorial* at the time *Eve's Film Review* was launched, so it is difficult to say how many cinemagoers would be aware of the print magazine. However, due to the longevity of the title (it was published weekly for over nine years) and its high production values I would suggest that it had a fairly big circulation. I think it is fair to suggest that the print and screen magazines would have been connected in the minds of many of the cinema audience.[24] Much of the feature content of *Eve the Lady's Pictorial* is shared by *Eve's Film Review*. The print magazine's main focus was on fashion, beauty and women's sports (usually traditionally male sports played by women such as football, golf and cricket); *Eve's Film Review* also featured these topics. As the two magazines share the name of *Eve*, I was interested to see if I could find a link between the print magazine and the cinemagazine in terms of ownership or editorial influence. Although I was unable to specifically connect *Eve the Lady's Pictorial* with Pathe personnel I would suggest that it is highly likely that the team that made *Eve's Film Review* was directly influenced by this namesake print magazine.[25]

That the screen magazine *Eve's Film Review* has much in common with its print counterpart *Eve the Lady's Pictorial* is clear. However, to gather together many ideas of womanhood, both these entertainments need to be considered within the even larger context of the pervasive use of the name Eve during the 1920s and early 1930s.

The Eternal Eve

During the period under review the sobriquet of Eve became a widely used shorthand to describe 'everywoman'. In reading contemporary newspapers and magazines Eve crops up everywhere. The name brought with it many associations, most of them echoing the contradictions inherent in Eve herself; in the beginning pure and innocent but ultimately too weak to resist temptation: **20**. This notion of the frailty of women in the face of temptation was often expressed in the mass media as a feminine lack of willpower in the face of objects of desire. For example, in a 1919 edition of *Eve* magazine an advertisement incorporates a letter from a woman called Joan who writes from Harrods' Ladies' Club: 'Dear Rosamund, There is an irresistible pulling at my purse-strings. I have been hypnotised by a rope of Harrods Ranee Pearls.'[26]

A different use of the name around this time revolved around ideas of Eve as the scheming temptress with power over men. A 1929 advertisement for Haig Whisky reads:

Eve et le serpent

IMP. LUMINEUSE
RADIANA (BTÉE S. G. L. G.)
PARIS (MADE IN FRANCE)

(20)
That 'come hither' look –
"Eve et le serpent' – postcard
(author's collection)

'The Temptation of Adam. The particular lure with which Eve tempted Adam to his fall will probably be argued about until the crack of doom. But there is only one lure that all the Eves – married or single – of all time can use with comparative certainty of success. If your Adam is restive, over tired, or recalcitrant, give him a glass of Haig Whisky. He will certainly fall to it.'[27]

The concept of Eve also became a way of expressing the feminine drive for *change* (Adam was quite happy for things in the Garden of Eden to remain just as they were). This advertisement for Heals in a 1920 issue of *Eve* expresses how this desire for change is transmuted into the quest for novelty in possessions:

'Eve is always ahead of the mode, a seeker after change. We remember how the original Eve overdid this to her undoing. But the beautiful, lively, modern things at Heals – fabric and furniture, pots and prints – are not forbidden fruit. On the contrary. Though quite as intriguing.'[28]

The feminine drive for change is most often translated into the impulse to transform the personal appearance by clothes or beauty products. Thus the notion of Eve became linked with female consumerism and in particular with the acquiring of those trappings which mark the feminine. Both women's magazines and *Eve's Film Review* are constantly introducing the 'new' and 'novel' in fashions, cosmetics and items for the home, suggesting that women must buy these products to avoid being old fashioned and by implication unattractive. The many films presenting innovations in fashion and accessories include: *Boots – Boots – Boots – Latest Russian Styles for Eve*, *A Camisole Novelty* and *Lady Nicotine's Latest*. The film *Trifles for Eve* introduces 'the latest gazinkas, oojahs and what-you-may-call-its for Eve, straight from Paris.' A rather sexy looking woman lies on a bed in a negligee flashing her stocking tops whilst she demonstrates the very latest of Eve's temptations. These are: the Laisy Daisy paper holder which allows you to smoke and eat chocolates whilst reading the paper (presumably); a cigarette dispenser, and a strange stuffed toy dog. *Newest Novelties* features the ultimate in laziness as a lady of leisure breaks off from flicking through a magazine to press the lever on a machine, which not only dispenses a cigarette but lights it too: **21** and **22**.

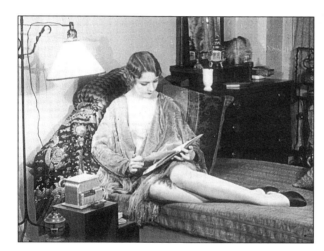

(21)
Time for a cigarette –
Newest Novelties

(22)
Have you got a light? –
Newest Novelties

(23)
Love stories for girls –
cover of Eve's Own Stories
26 March 1932

Woman as consumer became a notion with great currency in the 1920s. Man was seen as the earner, woman the shopper. A 1926 film directed by Howard Hawks entitled *Fig Leaves* features characters called Adam and Eve. Jeanne Thomas Allen writes of the film in terms of the depiction of Eve as a woman who must have 'pretty things' at all costs. In order to augment her wardrobe Eve takes a job as a haute couture mannequin, unbeknown to her husband. Eve's consumerist values 'are cast in terms of Original Sin: forbidden, guilt-inducing, titillating, and alluring' and Eve's yearning for new possessions is described as a case of the 'gimmes' when Adam says, 'Ever since you ate that apple, you've had the gimmes – first twin beds and now clothes.'[29] The difference between the sexes is expressed in terms of the woman's acquisitiveness, the drive to buy, buy, buy! *Fig Leaves* was well received by the trade press in Britain with *The Bioscope* critic calling it an 'Amusing comedy, illustrating woman's craving for clothes from the time of Eve to the present day.' However, we can see from the plot synopsis that adventurous Eve is eternally thwarted in her quest for a job and 'pretty things'. At the end of the film the critic observes that 'she sees the folly of her vanity and settles down to domestic felicity.'[30]

The character of 'Eve' is also found in many novels of the period, magazines such as *Eve's Own Stories*: **23** and stage plays including *The Curate's Egg*. An extract from this play was filmed for an edition of *Eve's Film Review* and features a couple portraying Adam and Eve on a stage set representing the Garden of Eden. Eve stretches up to grab an oversized apple which then opens up to reveal a treasure hidden inside – a beautiful dress, of course. Showgirls, models and celebrities are often enticed by the Pathe cameramen to eat an apple for *Eve's Film Review*: **24**; and intertitles such as 'Wonder if it's the apple that caused Adam so much trouble?' draw us to the significance of the act.[31]

In the 21st century 'Eve' as an icon continues to have resonance in the western world. In the April 2000 *Reality* magazine, James Sherwood celebrates snakeskin as a new fashion look: 'The Woman in snake is the new Eve. She's eaten the apple, killed the serpent and gone shopping.'[32] When television presenter Anthea Turner wanted an overhaul to undercut her goody-two-shoes image she posed naked for a magazine, draped in a snake. A women-only club called 'All About Eve' has recently been established in London, and a new glossy magazine for the modern woman, titled purely and simply *Eve*, just like its 1919 precursor, was launched in August 2000.

(24) Evelyn was tempted by an apple –
The Stars As They Are – Miss Evelyn Laye

Femininity as the Central Theme of *Eve's Film Review*

Women's magazines traditionally revolve around notions of the feminine. Articles in twenty-first century magazines such as *Cosmopolitan, Marie Claire* and the twenty-first century *Eve* have much in common with *Eve the Lady's Pictorial* and *Eve's Film Review*. There is a constant attention to the task of making oneself more beautiful, more feminine, with the implication that the result of these efforts will be the snaring of a man. Although the notion of the 'feminine ideal' can be seen as culturally constructed, within the woman's world of the glossy magazine its implications are understood. *Eve's Film Review* beauty tips featured in *Eyelashes While You Wait,* and reducing exercises such as *A Little Slimming a Day – Keeps the Avoirdupois Away* are presented as steps a woman should take in order to reach the 'feminine ideal'. An intertitle in the film *Shadow Shrinking Exercises No. 2* reads as follows: 'All Eves desiring to be supple, try this exercise – it will help you to acquire both grace and that "willowy" back'. A cheeky intertitle in *Slimming Drill* refers to the fashion for boyish figures: 'The only difference is, Adam concentrates on chests and Eve avoids them'.

The introduction from an early age to techniques of beautification and feminisation is well illustrated in *The Youngest Perm,* where an eighteen month old child is subjected to curlers and hairspray then given a mirror to admire her new look: 25. The idea of 'Eve' being obsessed with clothes and possessions is depicted in many *Eve's Film Review* items. Intertitles often express the notion that all women feel the same about glamorous fashions and accoutrements. In *The Parade – A New Fashion Note* an intertitle reads: 'This will make Eve's eyes glisten – a white satin gown with mink and ermine coatee **and** one hundred thousand pounds worth of emeralds and diamonds!' In *The Jewel Song* the rhetorical question is posed: 'Fine jewels – and fine raiment – was ever there such a tempting combination for Eve?'

The quest for a husband as a woman's main goal is less overtly expressed within women's magazines of today than those of earlier years. With the financial security offered by marriage in the 1920s and early 1930s, and the shortage of men to go around, perhaps it is not surprising that *Eve's Film Review* featured tips on flirtation (for example a film called *Signals*), and items about weddings (including *Here Comes the Bride – In Far Off Formosa*) and married life (such as *Wed-Time Stories* – a Joe Noble cartoon with hints for newlywed women on buying cuts of beef). Completing the picture of love and wedded bliss are the items on babies: *Just Babies…* for example which includes the intertitle: 'There's only one thing that attracts more of Eve's attention than a baby – a lot of them!' The implication here is that women love to see cute babies on screen, and intertitles – although in keeping with the general jokey tone – nevertheless respect the institution of motherhood. However, the incidence of items which celebrate the institutions of marriage and motherhood are relatively few in the grand scheme of *Eve's Film Review*. Most of the women featured are not shown as someone's wife or mother, but rather as individuals.

'Just the little what-nots that complete the how-de-does on Eve's little extras'[33]

In a time of 'two million superfluous women', anxiety for some women about attracting a mate would have precipitated a large market for goods purporting to increase their attractiveness. Whether this new attention to beauty and femininity was in fact constructed by the manufacturing industry, or was purely a result of demand or a reaction to the more austere war years is a matter open to debate. What is clear however, is that the 1920s and early 1930s saw an explosion of powder-puff culture.

The *Sunday Express* noted in 1931 that 1,500 lipsticks were being sold for every one that had been sold ten years earlier in 1921.[34] With the post-war increase in spending power for women in general, a new consumerism became possible.

(25) Learning to be pretty – The Youngest Perm

Women's magazines were full of advertisements for clothes, make-up and beauty products which augmented the already copious articles on the same subjects. There was a regular column within *Eve the Lady's Pictorial* called 'Eve Goes Shopping' and another called 'Powder Puff' which detailed novelties of dress and beauty products, listing manufacturers' names and prices. This kind of indirect advertising was also present in *Eve's Film Review* although prices were never quoted. The plethora of 'trifles', 'novelties' and 'gadgets' of the female wardrobe spotlighted by *Eve's Film Review* can be seen as an illustration of the rise of female consumerism. However *Eve's Film Review*, unlike its print contemporaries, claimed not to advertise particular products. In a letter dated 15 October 1928, W.A. Arthur of Pathe's Glasgow office reassures Frederick Watts that: 'we never use our "Pictorial", "Eve" or "Gazette" as an advertising medium'. In fact, this promise is not resolutely adhered to. Within fashion items in particular, companies were named. Lucille de Paris, Paul Caret, Maison Lewis, Jean Patou and Fourrures Max are a few of the many design houses mentioned by name within intertitles.[35] It is, however, possible that the names of well known designers were used to bring kudos to the cinemagazines rather than as direct advertisements, as most of the audience would not be in a financial position to purchase these clothes.

It can be claimed that the feminine drive to consume fashion and beauty products ad infinitum is a product of nurture rather than nature. Many feminists point the finger at capitalist culture creating a demand for products by introducing notions of inferiority within women, which they feel can only be cured by the acquisition of the latest beauty item. K. Sawchuk writes:

'Women's love of clothes, cosmetics, jewellery, their obsession with style and fashion reinforces the myth that we are narcissistic and materialistic. In turn this reinforces capitalism, which depends upon this obsession with our bodies for the marketing of new products.'[36]

However, it is equally possible to view an interest in fashion and beauty in a positive light. The lipstick, the high heel and the short skirt can be seen as tools of empowerment for women. It seems to me that the *pleasures* inherent in the purchase and use of these traditional markers of femininity, and by extension the reading about them and seeing them on the cinema screen, cannot be dismissed by the claim that they have been invented by men for the purpose of oppressing women. There is an element of *choice* which is often overlooked. Women can choose to take pleasure in the power of creativity; choosing what to wear and how to wear it rather than slavishly copying what they see on the screen. Likewise they can also choose to have no truck with fashion or beauty regimes at all.

Eve's Film Review can be situated as a close relative to the powder-puff culture of women's print magazines. Ideas about what constitutes the 'new woman' at any point in time are circulated through the mass media of the printed press, cinema, and now television and the internet. These ideas usually revolve around notions of femininity and how the 'new woman' rejects or modifies that which is considered the 'feminine ideal'. That *some* women in the 1920s and early 1930s were dressing in a more 'masculine' style, becoming more financially and sexually independent and infiltrating traditionally male domains such as the workplace and the football field, was obviously the source of anxiety to some commentators of the day. In the 1970s feminist discussions echoed many of the debates of the 1920s. Julia Kristeva argued that a revolution for women could only be achieved by 'calling attention at all times to whatever remains unsatisfied, repressed, new, eccentric, incomprehensible, disturbing to the status quo.'[37] It seems to me that many of the films within Eve's Film Review do just that by featuring outrageous, adventurous and sassy women. However, sometimes the images of these women seem to be undercut by jokey and dismissive intertitles.

'No sport is safe from her restless feet – not even football!'[38]
The Masculine Narration of *Eve's Film Review*
The question of who 'wrote' *Eve's Film Review* is an extremely interesting one. Unlike the print magazine, the 'author' of a particular item is not named. Of course, film is a collaborative medium and it is therefore not possible to name one person as the source of an item within *Eve's Film Review*. However, if we compare the cinemagazine for women with the print magazine for women, I think we can see a distinct difference in their respective styles of narration and terms of address.

The woman is silent in *Eve's Film Review*. Not only is her image controlled by the male film-makers, but her voice is controlled too. The 'narrator' of this cinemagazine is male. Although the images on screen frequently offer extremely positive representations of women, the jokey intertitles within *Eve's Film Review* often operate as an expression of male anxiety (echoing opinions appearing in the popular press of the time) at displays of feminine prowess.

The title of this section illustrates the mock outrage (of a man) that 'her' restless feet have dared to clothe themselves with football boots and enter the realm he traditionally regarded as 'safe' from women. If the narrator of *Eve's Film Review* had been posited as female (as I have suggested is the case within many women's print magazines for example) surely the intertitle would read, 'No sport is safe from *our* restless feet.' The title of this item, which shows women competing in several sports traditionally seen as 'male' including rowing and off-road motorcycling is *The Rival Sex*, positioning women as being in competition with men, although the images we see show women competing only against each other. As mentioned previously, the achievements of women on the sports field were often framed with titles that questioned the suitability of their efforts. *Are Women's Sports Too Strenuous?*, *Should Girls Box?* and *Is Eve Going Too Far?* are just three of many examples representative of this attitude.

That the expression of male anxiety is often clothed in a jokey pun on words may serve to lighten its impact. For example, in the film *A Woman Manned Fire Brigade* images of women firefighters are punctuated by the intertitle, 'Come to think of it, ladies should be experts in hose (and ladders)' – a joke relating to women's hosiery. Many of these comments provoke a good humoured groan. We *could* see these interjections as misogynist attempts to undermine women's achievements, but this is dangerous. We shouldn't forget that women have a sense of humour too and it is possible that the women of the time might have found these comments funny rather than detrimental.

Eve's Film Review was a unique space for showing both traditional femininity and its contemporary flip side; the 'emasculated' woman in a man's world. By virtue of its format as a variety magazine it could show potentially incongruous and contradictory items side by side. It could be argued that the makers of these films may have had a 'hidden agenda' which manifested itself in a jokey put-down of women's achievements by which they felt threatened, contrasted with a celebration of those things considered more suitable to a 'feminine' woman. However, claims of sexism and misogyny levelled at the film-makers seem to fall flat when the overwhelming impression given by these films is one of female power. Like the femme-fatale in 'film noir' whose strength is remembered after the film has ended even though she is usually tamed or killed during the denouement, the images of the resourceful, ambitious and exhibitionist women within *Eve's Film Review* stay with us long after we have laughed at the dismissive intertitles.

5 – For Ladies Only – Adam May Glance[1]
Specular Pleasure for Adam <u>and</u> Eve in *Eve's Film Review*

'We want … to see ourselves. We want to see on the screen the reflection, although not quite the humdrum reflection, of our homes and our lives, our sports and our pleasures. We want to see ourselves as we hope we look, as we think we might look, if our ships come home; ourselves in 'ideal' homes and 'ideal' costumes …'[2]

C.A. Lejeune is writing here specifically about the cinemagazine and the possible pleasures it might hold for the female viewer. These pleasures are spoken of in terms of a 'reflection' of a more perfect image of the female spectator, as if the screen were a mirror. Laura Mulvey details the fascination with likeness and recognition which is inherent in the experience of watching human forms on the cinema screen, and links this experience to the recognition by a child of its image in the mirror as a 'more complete, more perfect image.'[3]

The image of a perfectly made-up, glamorously dressed woman within the mise-en-scene of a prosperous household might be seen as the female spectator's ideal self. It seems to me that the idea of the perfect mirror image is illustrated most strongly within the many *Eve's Film Review* items in which the woman is shot in close-up to display hats or hairstyles. The framing of the head by the camera aperture and the direct look from the screen combine to suggest to the female spectator, a gaze into the mirror. In *The Crowning Glory – Latest Hair Styles, Hair Modes of the Moment* and *Bridal Veils for Wedding Belles* a woman looks directly into the camera and smiles, as any woman checking her look in the mirror might do: **26**. The direct look from the cinema screen by women within *Eve's Film Review* marks a special relationship with the female viewer, a relationship characterised by sameness as opposed to difference.

Looks into mirrors abound within *Eve's Film Review*, from the woman applying lipstick in *The Rival Sex* to the woman powdering her nose in *That Powder Puff*: **27**. As John Berger observes, the mirror in classical painting is often used as a symbol of the vanity of women.[4] The critical moral stance is undercut however by the fact that the woman looking at herself is often portrayed as actually

(26)
The camera as mirror –
Bridal Veils for
Wedding Belles

(27)
The vanity of women –
That Powder Puff

(28)
Looking at us looking at her –
Just – Hats

looking at the spectator. In *Eve's Film Review* the mirror image of the woman is often reflected as a look at the audience. In *Just – Hats* for example a woman looks into a mirror and her mirror image looks out of the mirror at us: **28**. The concept here is perhaps one of the woman looking into the mirror to see how she will look *to a man*. Berger writes of how woman from earliest childhood 'has been taught and persuaded to survey herself continually … because how she appears to others, and ultimately how she appears to men, is of crucial importance for what is normally thought of as the success of her life.'[5] This is a theme which runs through many beauty and fashion items and is perfectly illustrated in *The Youngest Perm*: **25** where the look into a mirror of an eighteen month old girl who has just had her hair permed is followed by the intertitle, 'Yvonne will have a lot more boyfriends after this!'

Eve's Tantalising Subjects

'In their traditionally exhibitionist role women are simultaneously looked at and displayed, with their appearance coded for strong visual and erotic impact so that they can be said to connote to-be-looked-at-ness.'[6]

That *Eve's Film Review* was aimed at the female audience is apparent from its promotion by Pathe and its choice of subject matter. However, even in a time where women outnumbered men by such a large amount it is obvious that any cinema audience will be made up of both sexes. That the male in the audience might find pleasure in the films within *Eve's Film Review* was acknowledged by the film-makers. Frederick Watts admitted: 'Incidentally, we know Adam has more than a sneaking regard for Eve's tantalising subjects that pass all too swiftly across the screen.'[7] Tantalising is an appropriate word to have been used here by the editor of *Eve's Film Review* as it seems to me that there is a great deal of tantalising going on for the benefit of the male spectators of this cinemagazine, and indeed for lesbian spectators.

The title of this chapter (taken from an *Eve's Film Review* item about swimsuits) offers the male spectator an interesting position. He is in the cinema, there is a magazine programme ostensibly made for women on the screen, this magazine is about 'women's things', it has not been made for his benefit. But, he likes it! Why shouldn't he enjoy looking at glamorous fashion parades, legs on display in a chorus line dance, or a famous crimper dressing women's hair? In fact, might he enjoy some of these things even more than the women they are supposedly on show for? The notion of a glance incorporates elements of furtiveness or even guilt; a quick look on the sly at something that we shouldn't really be looking at. The male spectator's interest in these films is sometimes acknowledged by the film-makers through intertitles. For example in the film *Fleet Footed Steps That 'Turned Up' At The New Oxford, London* an intertitle reads: 'A gentleman at the back says he missed a bit – could we slow it down a little. Certainly.' There then follows slow motion footage of dancer Anita Elson jumping up and down flashing her bloomers. The idea that men might look at *Eve's Film Review* in a different way to women is particularly interesting in view of the fact that many of its items contain elements of the erotic.

'With so much silk-clad ankle about nowadays, one can hardly blame the mud spots for clinging to Eve's stockings'[8]
Fetishisation Within *Eve's Film Review*
That femininity is the central theme of *Eve's Film Review* is, I believe, unquestionable. There is a strong sense of fascination by the film-makers as to what makes a woman *different* from a man. Sigmund Freud wrote about fetishism as early as 1914 in an article entitled 'A Case of Foot-Fetishisation'. The works of Freud were very much 'in vogue' in Britain during the 1920s as a result of more of his articles being translated into English at this time. His ideas had been introduced to the popular consciousness through debate in newspapers and women's magazines and may have influenced the makers of *Eve's Film Review*. I feel it is valid to consider Freud's work here due to the proliferation of fetish objects within the films and the style in which these objects are portrayed.

'... the foot or shoe owes its preference as a fetish – or part of it – to the circumstances that the inquisitive boy peered at the woman's genitals from below, from her legs up; fur and velvet – as has long been suspected – are a fixation of the sight of pubic hair, which should have been followed by the longed-for sight of the female member; pieces of underclothing, which are so often chosen as a fetish, crystallise the moment of undressing, the last moment in which the woman could still be regarded as phallic.'[9]

The shoe, (and by implication the foot), that most revered of all fetish objects, often featured in early 'erotic' films such as *The Gay Shoe Clerk* (1903) and is a regular star guest in the *Eve's Film Review* experience. *New Heels for Old*, *Shoes Who* and *Shoe Shows* all offer a chance for the sight of a pretty ankle: **29**. Legs by extension are much on display, either in the many 'high-kick' revue extracts, or in fashion items which use novelties – such as garters which secrete tiny powder puffs (*M'Lady's Garter*), a new style of spattees (*Scotland v Russia*), or button up rubber stocking protectors (*Cheating the Mud Spots*) – to justify long lingering looks at ladies' legs: **30**. Beauty parade films often focus on legs rather than faces: **31**. Velvet and fur feature in many of the fashion items including *Fur Novelty* which shows a variety of fur garters: **32** and *Here Come the Bridesmaids' Dresses* where a sumptuous velvet dress with a tight-fitting bodice, cowl neck and puffed sleeves is modelled. In an item entitled *Fur Fashions* three women who model fur coats look seductively at the camera/audience as they pull up the sumptuous fur

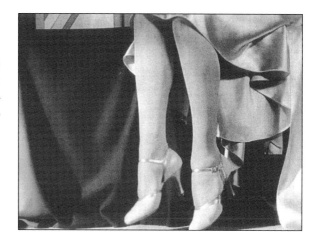

(29)
Remember it's a
shoe show –
Shoes Who

(30)
Long lingering looks
at ladies' legs –
Cheating the Mud Spots

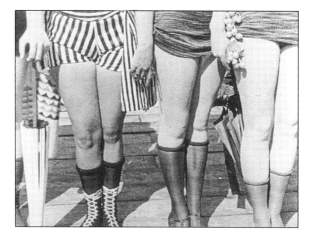

(31)
Beauty parade –
Costumes for the Peaches
on the Beaches

collars around their necks and turn to display the coats: **33**. The sensuousness of these fabrics and the mysteries they conceal underneath is often emphasised by intertitles such as: 'This coat of black cloth and civit cat appears quite simple but a wonderful orientalised jumper of white velvet with jewelled embroidery lurks beneath', and a cloak is described as a 'gorgeous cape in panne velvet shielding a creation in crepe georgette.'[10]

Items featuring underclothing include, *Brevities, Latest Parisian Lingerie* and *A Camisole Novelty* and the women who model the latest in lingerie often look seductively at the camera: **34**. Occasionally a spurious storyline is used to justify the removal of undergarments; in *Lines of the Times* for example the subject matter of the film is how much easier it is for the modern woman on wash day now that her undies are skimpier than her grandmammas: **35** and **36**. There is also a fascination with the ornaments and accoutrements a woman makes use of to mark her difference. *The Latest in Hair Adornments, The Language of a Fan* and *The Coquettish Mantilla – and How to Wear It* are just a few examples of the many items dedicated to feminine accessories. The body is often fragmented within *Eve's Film Review* allowing other parts of the body to be fetishised along with legs and feet. Items include: *The Latest in London – Not 'Arf Bad, Either* (designs painted on a woman's shoulder) and *Glad to See Your Back Again* – a beauty contest where judges choose the most beautiful back.

Even if we don't agree with Freud's theories about fetishism, the abundance of shots of feet, ankles, legs and female flesh in general within *Eve's Film Review* is quite astounding. However, this *could* be seen merely as an indication of what film-makers were able to 'get away with' at the time, from the point of view of wishing to titillate male viewers. *Eve's Film Review* was not subject to the same rules of censorship as feature films of the period as it was classified as 'news' and therefore exempt.

"Seeing Sights in the Sierras"
Extraordinary Displays of Sexuality Within *Eve's Film Review*
Displays of female sexuality burst out all over the screen in *Eve's Film Review*. Of course, the use of the female body as a sexual spectacle has been a major feature of cinematic entertainment since its very beginning. Proto-cinema devices such as the Kinetoscope and its 'What the Butler Saw' type stories often involved the display of the female body for the pleasure of the viewer. Early films such as *Trapeze Disrobing Act* (1901) carried through this tradition and I believe that *Eve's Film Review* became its apotheosis. As a cinematic format outside the rules and boundaries of the feature film, the cinemagazine could focus on the body of the woman as the locus of specular pleasure without being forced to bind the spectacle into a narrative. The woman is not a character with hopes, fears, motivations or goals as she may be in the narrative film, she *can* be there merely

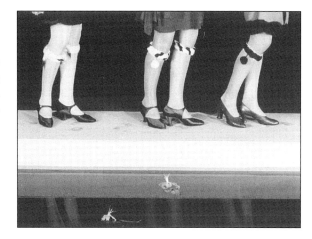

(32)
The latest short-skirt
adjuncts –
A Fur Novelty

(33)
Sumptuous and
sensuous fur coats –
Fur Fashions

(34)
Addressing
the spectator –
Brevities

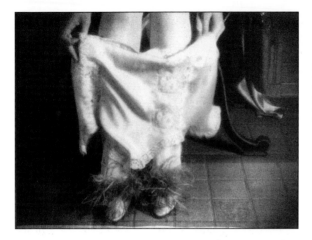

(35)
How much easier
it is with silk undies –
Lines of the Times

(36)
You can just wash
them out in the sink –
Lines of the Times

(37)
Fancy an orange? –
Citrus

'to-be-looked-at'. The fashion mannequin, the dancer and the chorus girl are all by profession 'on display' and as they are the kind of women who claim the majority of screen time in *Eve's Film Review* they can be seen to reinforce the position of women as spectacle within this cinemagazine.

Eve's Film Review shares many conventions used by early pornographic/erotic films such as the use of the pretext of a theatrical performance to place the body on display. Many items from stage revues of the time are filmed for the cinemagazine and particularly favoured are lines of chorus girls in 'leg-shows' performing 'high-kicks'. As previously mentioned, displays of women's legs were often filmed from a 'worms-eye view' and a girl up a ladder was a favourite subject: **37** and **38**. However, unlike the narrative film which often uses the device of the show-girl to unite the look of the audience with the look of the on-screen protagonist, the audiences for the 'leg-shows' within *Eve's Film Review* are never seen. This opens a space for women's pleasure in these displays of the female body that I will examine later in this chapter.

The absence of a need to display the female body within the context of a narrative means that *Eve's Film Review* can also place women on display in milieus other than the theatrical. Constance Balides has illustrated the increasing use of everyday situations in early films (women walking in the street or shoe shopping for example) as space for displaying women's sexuality.[11] She links this tendency to the expanded presence of women in public places during the late 19th and early 20th centuries. This seems to me an interesting conjecture and looking at *Eve's Film Review* in the light of this theory proves enlightening. Rather than showing women in everyday or ordinary situations to foreground the sexual nature of women's public presence, *Eve's Film Review* tends to show women in *extraordinary* situations with the same results. In the period under consideration, women were becoming increasingly visible *everywhere*, including traditionally male territories. The cinemagazine in its never-ending quest for the novel, with its place outside the exigencies of verisimilitude adhered to by the feature, could show women in all sorts of bizarre situations for the purpose of titillation. For example the item *Seeing Sights in the Sierras* features a group of women climbing mountains and frolicking around oil rigs in bathing costumes. That these women are probably chorus-girls is evidenced by the fact that they do high-kicks on the mountain side. The oil rig setting provides an excellent opportunity for some 'artistic' shots of the girls' legs amongst the phallic iron structures: **39** and some astounding shots of the girls climbing the rigs from below: **40**. Another group of showgirls is seen picking oranges in *Citrus* – in their swimsuits of course: **37**. In a particularly nice sequence there is a moving shot from a lorry travelling through the orange groves; views of girls standing on ladders picking fruit are framed with a woman's leg in the foreground: **41**. The film ends with a shot of a girl emerging from a huge pile of oranges, the

(38)
A worm's eye view –
Citrus

(39)
Tableaux vivants –
Seeing Sights
in the Sierras

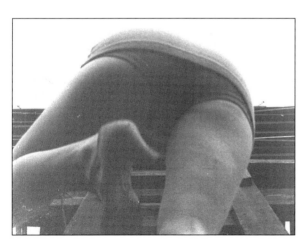

(40)
Seen from below –
Seeing Sights
in the Sierras

impression given is that she is naked. The intertitle that introduces this shot reads simply 'Fruity': **42**.[12]

The pictorial quality of some of the images within *Seeing Sights in the Sierras* is reminiscent of 'tableaux vivants' ('living pictures'); theatrical displays of female bodies in stationary poses popular in music hall, burlesque shows and supper clubs. Interestingly, the trade show organised by Pathe to launch *Eve's Film Review* featured tableaux vivants of 'Eve and her daughters through the ages'. It was suggested to exhibitors that they might precede their screenings of *Eve's Film Review* with similar tableaux, '… an enterprising showman who seized upon the idea would undoubtedly please his audience by striking a new note.'[13] *Seeing Sights in the Sierras* acknowledges its intentions to titillate the audience by

(41)
Arty shots –
Citrus

(42)
Fruity shots –
Citrus

65

intertitles such as, 'Giving the drills a thrill' before a shot of girls being spun around on a piece of drilling machinery: **43**. The item has no discernible 'story' or theme other than the beauty of the female form (there is no connection made between the shots on the mountainside and the shots around the oil rigs) and the item is not about the clothes these women wear, as the bathing suits are not described in intertitles as is the norm for fashion items. The *raison d'etre* of this item is to show scantily clad women in various tableaux and diverse states of action for the pleasure of the spectator. This raises interesting questions about who exactly was the intended spectator for this item, and for other items which also use women purely and simply as erotic spectacle.

When the Woman Looks

'In our society men can and do stare – at women. It is a look which confers a mastery. It represents a right to access, pass judgment and initiate or invite on the basis of that judgment. Women do not stare at people in this way, we are not the subjects of the look but the objects.'[14]

Rosalind Coward has explored the relationships women have with photographs and concludes that although it is not socially acceptable for a woman to stare at others in our society (in the street for example), she can stare at photographs for as long as she likes. It seems to me that this possibility is even stronger within the darkened privacy of the cinema auditorium. Social niceties are dispensed with and the captive audience can, and do, stare.

Much work has been done on the importance of 'the look' within 'classical Hollywood cinema'. Most important to my discussion here is the debate set in motion by Laura Mulvey in her article 'Visual Pleasure and Narrative Cinema', which posited the view that the male look was dominant within narrative cinema. When a male character looks at a woman within a narrative film, we are invited to take his position as 'bearer of the look' (whether we are of the same gender or not); we identify with him and he becomes our on-screen surrogate and mediator of our look. The woman is *unaware* of the look of the cinema audience. That is to say that the world which she inhabits is constructed in such a way that she *appears* not to know that she is being looked at, except by characters within the diegesis.

Mulvey's initial work left little space for women's pleasure in narrative cinema; however, she has since re-evaluated her conclusions and others have expanded upon her ideas or offered new positions for female spectators. Even so, Mulvey's original conclusions about the power of the on-screen look by a male protagonist form an interesting starting point to investigate the specificities of the look within *Eve's Film Review*.

(43)
Giving the drills a thrill –
Seeing Sights in the Sierras

Eve's Film Review is a women's world where men seldom appear except as dance partners, entertainers and hairdressers. Unlike the classical Hollywood narrative which almost without fail involves a complex interaction of looks between male and female characters, within *Eve's Film Review* there is no male mediator of the look. It is as if the woman defines herself. There is of course the cameraman, the film editor and Mr Watts who decide what the audience will see, but the power of the woman-centered image unmediated by the look of an on-screen male shines through. In around 1500 *Eve's Film Review* items held by Pathe only a handful of these involve an on-screen look by a man at a woman;[15] two such items being *They're Off!* and *Eve in the Swim.* Although both these films are atypical of the scopic situation within *Eve's Film Review* by the very presence of a male look on screen, they reveal much in their use of earlier erotic traditions whilst still remaining outside the structures of the classical Hollywood narrative form.

The first of these items falls into the category of the 'Peeping Tom' film defined by Tom Gunning.[16] This involves a point-of-view shot mediated by some kind of device – a telescope or keyhole for example. *They're Off!* illustrates how a woman can take her clothes off underwater. The intertitle which precedes the disrobing seems to offer a justification for the display as it attracts the attention of the spectator: 'Watch this – it might be handy if you happen to sit on a wasp's nest'. After the woman has stripped to her swimsuit a title reads: 'Visitors to this unique crystal-clear lake are about as private as goldfish in a bowl.' We are then shown two men looking through a glass-bottomed boat followed by a shot of a woman swimming underneath them framed by the 'window'. Here the woman does not acknowledge the look and the men are not 'punished' for their voyeurism as they would be in many of the earlier incarnations of this type of film. This seems to condone their peep-show pleasure. *They're Off!* shares the conventions of earlier risqué films such as *Pull Down the Curtains, Suzie* (1904) where the woman undressing does not see the man who is watching her. The on-screen voyeur is a surrogate for the man in the audience who is also watching without being seen in the darkened privacy of the cinema auditorium. However, *They're Off* differs from the earlier undressing film in that the voyeurs are not seen in the same frame as the woman they are watching. This perhaps leaves a space for the female cinema spectator to enjoy the spectacle of a scantily clad woman swimming underwater, without her look being mediated by that of a man: **44**.

The second example of the on-screen male look is found in the item *Eve in the Swim*, a complex and extremely interesting item about how the size of women's bathing costumes has shrunk over the years. As well as offering the spectator scopophilic pleasure through camera tricks which superimpose three images of the same woman in progressively skimpier swimsuits upon a black background: **45** the film draws attention to the process of cinema itself. As the mannequin turns slowly to display her bathing suit and by implication her body, there is a shot of a bell-boy (who has earlier taken the dressing gown which the model has removed to reveal her swimsuit) looking directly at the camera with his mouth open as if mesmerised by the erotic spectacle before him: **46**. He is punished for his look by the cameraman,[17] who we then see cranking the handle of the camera and smiling at the bathing belle. The implication here is that the boy is 'too young' to enjoy the woman as spectacle, but the cameraman and by implication the grown man in the cinema audience are acknowledged as suitable voyeurs. However, what makes this item different from *They're Off!* and more akin to the vast majority of *Eve's Film Review* items is the look of the woman. The woman on display looks at the camera, and by implication at the spectator.

The look from a character on screen directly at the audience is an exhibitionist look, it is a 'showing off' look which says, 'look at me – I am showing you something'. In many instances within *Eve's Film Review* the look says, 'look at me – I am showing you the latest shoes, frocks, bathing suits' and this can easily be read as 'look at me – I am showing you my legs, body, flesh.' Thus the woman who takes a Turkish Bath in the item *The Weigh of All Flesh (Eliminator!)* seems to be addressing a male spectator when she is shown giggling and throwing her head back in the bath coquettishly. She is tucked up in a blanket with steam rising all around her – she purses her lips and opens her eyes wide as she mimes extreme excitement and enjoyment. The suggestion is of sexual pleasure. Her look into the camera is a conspiratorial look, as if to say, 'Yes, you shouldn't really be watching me having a Turkish Bath, it is naughty – this is for women to watch!': **47**. Whilst I agree that this direct address may carry an erotic charge for the male spectator, I would suggest that the woman on screen is also addressing the female spectator but in a different way.

(44)
Seen through a glass
bottomed boat –
They're Off

(45)
Seeing more and
more of Eve –
Eve in the Swim

(46)
Mesmerised –
Eve in the Swim

(47)
Gosh it's hot in here –
The Weigh of All Flesh
(Eliminator!)

Women's Pleasure in the Female Body as Spectacle

'... even if it is admitted that the woman is frequently the object of the voyeuristic or fetishistic gaze in the cinema, what is there to prevent her from reversing the gaze for her own pleasure?'[18]

If we believe that cross-gender identification occurs within the cinema then it is possible (and I think probable) that female spectators could enjoy the spectacle of the woman's body on display in the same way as a male spectator. There is obviously great potential pleasure in these films for lesbian spectators. Heterosexual women of the period might also have experienced the same frisson at the sight of female sexuality on the screen, a sense of forbidden pleasure.

Mary Ann Doane's work on 'Film and the Masquerade' is mostly concerned with narrative cinema and the possibilities for women of trans-sex identification in assuming the role of the dominant male character within the diegesis. This idea is interesting when looking at *Eve's Film Review* in that it gives the female viewer an opportunity to take the male spectatorial position in *desiring* the woman on screen rather than merely desiring *to be* the woman on screen. If we agree with Rosalind Coward's contention that it is acceptable within our society for men to stare but not for women to actively look, the cinema provides a unique space for women to break the taboo of staring. In the darkened cinema they are 'allowed' to stare at men on screen, and more importantly here, at other women.

It seems to me that the direct address by the on-screen woman seen in films such as *The Weigh of All Flesh (Eliminator!)* is the locus of an *extra* kind of pleasure for the female spectator. This specifically female pleasure is suggested by Judith

Mayne as she describes the denouement of *What Happened in the Tunnel* (1903) where a man attempts to kiss a woman in the dark, only to find that he has kissed her maid by mistake: '… if the two women in this film are objects of the male look, they turn the tables by laughing at the man. Metaphorically speaking their laughter, the film's punch line, suggests a flouncing skirt or a movement of the female body that resists the authority of the male look.'[19] Mayne does not mention in her account of the film that the maid looks at the camera, but Miriam Hansen draws attention to this fact: 'the maid's direct glance at the camera suggests not only that she was not merely a prop but that she, rather than her mistress, might have authorised the substitution.'[20] Thus the look here holds the implication of power and is an acknowledgement of who is in control of this situation. If we consider again the item, *The Weigh of All Flesh (Eliminator)*, we can see that the woman's look to camera makes it clear she knows she is being watched. She laughs and smiles at the camera in a cheeky acknowledgment that she is being looked at whilst squirming around in a bath. From the point of view of the female spectator, this look carries extra power. As Miriam Hansen describes the look to the camera in *What Happened in the Tunnel* (1903):

'By putting the representation in quotation marks, as it were, the female performer at once enacts traditional norms of femininity (including their pornographic violation) and displays them as cultural conventions. So even when the woman is reduced to an object of prurient anticipation, the performer's glance at the camera may add a twist to an otherwise sad joke.'[21]

The direct look from the woman on screen may suggest invitation, flirtation and sexual availability to the male spectator, but perhaps this direct look works differently for a female spectator. Perhaps this self-conscious look is an acknowledgement to the female spectator that the woman on screen knows *exactly* what she is doing. She is performing, she is on display, she is a spectacle, she knows she is being watched and she likes it, she is ultimately in control. The direct look of a woman on display can therefore be an expression of female power.

John Berger investigates the direct look at the painter/viewer by women within paintings of the classical period and concludes that the passive, languid look common within works of art is an address to the spectator which connotes the availability of the woman. He also identifies this look within print pornography. The cinema has the advantage of movement over paintings and magazine photographs. The smiles, winks and 'flouncing of skirts' that accompany the direct look at the audience within *Eve's Film Review* can be seen as transgressing this notion of passivity. *Eve's Film Review* is a space where women can actively express their sexuality: by dancing, by showing their legs and by taking Turkish Baths.

"The only item missing is – ? (Guess it, Adam!)"[22]

Whilst the on-screen look of a man at a woman is very rare within *Eve's Film Review* there are many examples of women looking at other women. This is most obvious in fashion items where women display clothes for each other, either in a catwalk situation where the woman in the cinema audience could feel herself to be part of the elite fashion show audience, or in a situation where models show each other their latest outfits.

The second scenario, featuring the exchange of looks between women, occurs within films which focus on real female friendship (rather than models posing as friends). Perhaps at a time of 'two million surplus women' this is not surprising. Many items feature women going on holiday without men and playing sport, obviously enjoying each other's company. These looks tend to be prompted by the novelty of being filmed; girls look at each other and laugh. These looks could be thought of as supportive looks rather than the judgmental looks sometimes seen in the fashion items.

The on-screen look of a woman at a man is probably the rarest interaction of looks within *Eve's Film Review*. It is interesting to note the lack of the figure of the male as erotic object within these films, especially as the early 1920s saw the trend of the matinée idol. In the case of Rudolph Valentino in particular, male stars offered the display of their sexuality through the cinema as a possible pleasure for women. However, recent research including Jackie Stacey's book: *Star-gazing: Hollywood Cinema and Female Spectatorship*[23] suggests that women often claim female film stars for idols and prefer to watch female rather than male film stars. *Eve's Film Review* only very occasionally acknowledged the attraction of the male idol. There are a few examples of overt masculinity in the exhibition dancing items, in particular during the 'apache' dance sequences where brawny men throw women over their shoulders or dash them to the ground. These passionate and sexy items often have the iconography of the Middle East, filmed in studio sets which are piled high with opulent Moorish fabrics and cushions: **48**. Presumably these settings would bring to mind the 'sex' novel and 'exotic' films such as the Valentino vehicle *The Sheik* (1921). The 'apache' dance sequences are a stunning representation of the brute force of man and no doubt set many hearts a-flutter in the cinemas of the day. However, they are atypical of *Eve's Film Review* where, on the whole, men are conspicuous by their absence. Perhaps this is due to the fact that the film-makers believed that women preferred to see their like on screen. If they took their lead from women's print magazines of the day they would have found that the vast majority of images featured were those of women. Perhaps they were thinking more of their male viewers and were of the opinion that, 'man is reluctant to gaze at his exhibitionist like'.[24]

Girl Power

'I do not believe that a beautiful woman being looked at is 'passive' beneath the 'male gaze'. I feel that that is a distortion. It's not correct. I'd rather think of it in terms of the Helen of Troy motif, that is, a woman in the glory of her sexuality.'[25]

Camille Paglia is one of the most outspoken feminists currently tackling the issue of a woman's 'to-be-looked-at-ness'. Laura Mulvey's early conclusions about the domineering look of the male are being re-evaluated within film studies and within the wider sphere of the study of popular culture. Paglia elevates pop icon Madonna to the status of 'the true feminist' due to her exhibitionism, ambition and sexual self-awareness. Like many of the women within *Eve's Film Review* Madonna flaunts her sexuality, acknowledges the look of the spectator with looks of her own and actively enjoys being on display. We cannot deny that some women take pleasure in being looked at by both men and other women.

Within some current feminist writing a rejection of the all-encompassing power of the male gaze is coupled with a reclamation of women's pleasures in fashion and beauty. Early critiques of cosmetics and clothes were usually reductive and moralistic, claiming fashion to be analogous to enslavement and a patriarchal tool of oppression. More recent work is engaged in finding a new position for women whereby our pleasures in fashion and beauty need not be at odds with our feminism. The question is posed, 'What if self decoration gives women a sense of potency to act in the world?'[26] It seems that the days when a 'real' feminist could not wear lipstick are over: women are at liberty to enjoy fashion and make-up whatever their political convictions.

(48)
Death through passion –
Terpsichore

(49)
Hello boys –
Seeing Sights
in the Sierras

It seems to me that most feminist criticism about images of women in film deny both the female performer and the female spectator the possibilities of self-awareness and pleasure in displays of the female body. The cinemagazine's retention of elements of the 'cinema of attractions' allows it greater freedom to break the conventions generally adhered to by narrative cinema. The direct address to the camera allows the woman on screen a great deal of power. It suggests that she is in control of her own sexuality and is having fun flirting with the camera, the cameraman, and by implication the audience. This expression of sexuality on screen can be seen as being related to changes within society at the time *Eve's Film Review* was made, including the growing visibility of women's sexuality through dress and behaviour being vociferously discussed in the popular press of the time. I recognise that the free expression of sexuality was not possible for every woman due to constraints of age, religion, family and morality. Nevertheless *Eve's Film Review* provided an opportunity for vicarious enjoyment of expressions of female sexuality for many different kinds of women in the cinema audience.

Far from being passive objects of the male gaze, for me the women within *Eve's Film Review* are typified in the final moments of *Seeing Sights in the Sierras*. Shot from above a woman climbs a vertiginous oil rig, looking up and directly into the camera until the whole of the screen is full of her broad grin of obvious enjoyment: **49**. This sequence may have been shot with the male spectator in mind (it follows the 'worm's eye view' shot mentioned earlier): **40** however it is obvious that the woman being filmed is 'a woman in the glory of her sexuality.'[27] Her pleasure in being looked at is apparent and that allows me, as a female spectator, to enjoy the spectacle too.

6 – An Overview of the Films

As *Eve's Film Review* is rarely seen today, a descriptive review of examples together with frame enlargements from the actual films, has been included here. I have designated eight main categories. Of course, some of the films cross boundaries and some fall outside them, but I hope the following will provide an insight into the main themes.

'Who does Eve dress for? Herself or Adam?'[1] Fashion Items

Without a doubt, the fashion item predominates within *Eve's Film Review*. Flicking through print magazines of the 1920s is a feast for the eyes, with line drawings of drop-waisted sportswear and beaded dancing dresses making the mouth water. Seeing flapper frocks actually move on the cinema screen is even better. Cinemagoers of the 1920s could drool over the gorgeous outfits of their favourite female stars shimmying past them in feature films. They could also take a more leisurely look at fashion items within *Eve's Film Review* as every week the very latest would be paraded past them, often in glorious stencil colour.[2]

The earliest fashion items within *Eve's Film Review* follow the style of their predecessors of the 1910s. They are mostly straightforward presentations of the latest designer outfits in a set representing a domestic interior; usually a drawing room. Mannequins turn their bodies displaying the fabric and cut of their gowns, looking directly into the camera. Extremely expensive coats are often unbuttoned and dropped on the floor in a 'couldn't care less how much it cost' manner. Long-shots showing whole outfits are usually intercut with close-ups of details such as embroidery or accessories. In *The Verdict of Paris* for example, a close-up shows the beading detail on a long Paul Caret dress after an intertitle proclaiming 'Linger longer frocks!' In *Cloaks and Toques* a series of silk and velvet 'Batik Française' tea-gowns and evening cloaks is presented. After long-shots of models holding out their arms to show the cut of the large sleeves, a close-up shows more clearly the ornate designs of the fabrics.

Two women friends often admire each others' outfits in these fashion presentations. In *Parisian Capes and Shapes* an elaborately dressed woman enters screen left wearing a cloak trimmed with monkey fur. She shakes hands with her

(50) Showing off to a friend – Parisian Capes and Shapes

(51) Admiring her look in the mirror – M'Lady's Dress While She Waits

hostess, who admires her friend's outfit as she twirls around a few times before casting off her cloak and flopping into an armchair: **50**. The hostess stands up to pour two glasses of wine, giving her a chance to do a little posing herself. A close-up of her visitor follows, to show details of her hat and short-sleeved dress with monkey fur sleeve trim. In their Maison Georgette outfits the pair seem rather elaborately dressed for a girls' gossip session, but why not?

The setting of these films sometimes implies that the cinemagoer is in the position of purchaser at a design house or boutique. The viewer is being presented with the fashions as if she is in a salon or showroom. Sometimes an on-screen representative admires or touches the clothes. In *La Mode – In Paris* for example, a man and woman sit stage left as two models walk through swing doors as if from a dressing room. They spin on their heels and the man turns to consult with his wife as a vendeuse makes notes of the items they wish to purchase.

Far more women made their own clothes in the 1920s and 1930s than do so today, and print magazines provided sewing tips and paper patterns. Some, such as *Newest Fashions – Leach's Family Dressmaker* (published between 1921 and 1925), were devoted to helping the modern woman run up copies of the latest modes on her sewing machine at home. Pathe made claims that their fashion films would provide women with inspiration for home sewing. This quote from *The Film Renter and Moving Picture News* illustrates the idea that women might take notes in the cinema to use later in designing their own outfits:

'Close views of sartorial productions will be included in the woman's film, which will provide kinema going Eves with animated patterns which can be copied. Fashions in hats, handbags, sunshades, footwear and other feminine vanities will flicker across the screen, and we may yet see the arrival of the period when women will descend on kinemas equipped with notebooks in which to record the ideas they glean from these animated fashions.'[3]

Inspiration is provided by women who make their own clothes. In the film *Camera Interviews – Mrs Arthur Hamilton The Swimmer* we are shown several examples of the ornate swimming costumes designed and made by the cross channel aspirant as she poses around her beach hut. There are many films showing millinery techniques that women could use in their own homes for creating or trimming beautiful hats.

Women are often seen in fashion items looking in full-length mirrors – this is a handy technique for showing both the front and the back of the dress at the same time (for example in *M'Lady's Dress While She Waits*: **51**). A picture frame device is often used to surround shots of women modelling hats or jewellery. In the film *For Milady's Hair – A Fashion Note* for example two women model headbands which, says the hairdresser Emile, complement the shingle hairstyle. In one shot the model actually places her hand onto the frame, showing that she is standing behind a cutout rather than this effect being achieved by a camera mask: **52.** The title of films using this framing device is often 'Living Paintings', emphasising the pictorial quality of many of the shots and the fact that the medium of cinema can bring static images to life. In the constant search for new and novel ways to present fashion items to the cinemagoer Pathe used all manner of settings and techniques. Two of the most remarkable are *In Fashion's Train* where models give a 'Pullman Parade' aboard a moving locomotive, and *F-A-S-H-I-O-N and How Eve Spells It – an Idare Fantasy* in which shots of glorious outfits are linked by a poem through intertitles.

Print magazines of the twenties such as *Paris Modes* (published between 1923 and 1927) celebrated the chic French designs lusted after by many British women. *Eve's Film Review* also looked towards the French capital for its fashion stories. Many items were exchanged with the French branch of the company or bought in from freelance filmmakers. Titles include: *Fashions A La Parisienne* (Maison Clé evening wear is modelled); *The Verdict of Paris* (announcing the longer skirt length); *The Latest from Paris for Eve* (new hairstyles and cute hats); *Mermaid Modes from Paris* (swim-wear); and *Furs and a Frock from Paris* (Fourrures Max coats and a Maison Valentine white silk afternoon dress). The vagaries of Dame Fashion are always described in tones which suggest that Pathe is presenting its viewers with the very latest, the most up to date, hot off the sewing machine models. Items are described as 'the latest Paris notion' and the greatest compliment for a hat, gown or handbag seems to be that it is 'très chic'.

The intertitles describing the fabrics and colours of clothes take much from the style of magazine articles of the time. Language is often elaborate and excessive as attempts are made to verbalise the textures and patina of certain items. A bride's dress in *Miss José Collins* is described as: 'A queenly wedding dress of white georgette lavishly embroidered with diamante. The square sleeves support gleaming tassels.' In *Frocks Furs and Furbelows* a beautiful gown is introduced with the intertitle: 'This 'Hockley' sealing-wax red frock of lace and crepe de chine, sets the seal of fashion on wide sleeves, slashed open from wrist to elbow.' Alliteration and onomatopoeia are often used to give an impression of the feel of fabrics, for example: 'Every Eve must plead guilty at some time or another to a longing for furs – soft, sleek and snug.'[4] Fur coats would have been out of reach for many working class girls in the 1920s, and an item called *Foxy* might have given them an idea for acquiring a coat that didn't involve saving up for years or finding a sugar daddy. Viewers are told: 'Some of the girls have formed the "Get

(52)
Pretty as a picture –
For Milady's Hair –
A Fashion Note

(53)
In the arms today… –
Foxy

Yourself a Silver Fox" Club' before shots of a group of women walking in the countryside with fox cubs on leads. When shown to twenty-first century audiences it takes a while for the real meaning of the film to sink in, but when the club motto appears on screen after shots of women cuddling fox cubs: **53** the message is clear: 'In the arms now, around the neck some day!'

The elaborate style of description used in these fashion items and the posturing of models was the subject of an amusing parody in an early 1920s *Pathe Pictorial* item. Although *Pathe Pictorial* was ostensibly the boys' version of *Eve's Film Review* (featuring transport stories, men at work and male sports) the reel never featured serious fashion stories.[5] In *Fashion Forecasts for Men by Mr Leslie Henson* the popular comedian models some outrageously silly menswear. One outfit is designed for the racecourse and features an enormous striped bow tie and extremely wide checked jacket: **54**. An intertitle reads: 'The coat opens easily, thus allowing rapid access to pockets for use of bookmakers ...' Leslie moves the bottom of the coat and a man offscreen puts his hand in Leslie's trouser pocket and takes out a wad of cash. Another intertitle predicts: 'High-necked jackets in thick mackintosh will be all the rage for spaghetti and asparagus parties (This saves hosing down after meals)'. Leslie makes a meal of eating some asparagus spears before modelling some tennis wear and a golfing outfit with hugely padded jacket and very wide plus fours. The implications of Leslie's overblown posturing and the style of the titling is that fashion is obviously a women's pleasure and not for the serious, masculine male. Men might secretly enjoy watching women's fashion being paraded across the screen but it would be quite a different matter for a regular men's fashion film to be shown.

Within *Eve's Film Review*, jokes are often made at the expense of men in the cinema audience. That the 'Adams' accompanying their 'Eves' to the cinema could never understand the vagaries of fashion is a frequent topic as this *Cloaks and Toques* intertitle illustrates: 'And the feathers on these latest "Maison Lewis" toques, (by the way, Adam, what **is** a toque?) make a little hat go a long way.' Husbands are often mentioned as the possible source of money for some of the outfits on display. The implication is usually that a husband must provide for his wife's fripperies and frocks and that he does so reluctantly but is always pleased with the result. After a shot of a husband looking outraged at his wife's dress bills in the film *Creations*, an intertitle reads: 'But, even Adam will admit this "Maison Lewis" white duvetyn sports hat (and scarf) embroidered with kid grapes, is chic'.

That men would sometimes enjoy fashion items as much as their female companions was often acknowledged within *Eve's Film Review*. Parades of sexy dresses, feminine underpinnings, hosiery and footwear were often presented with a knowing aside that addressed the male spectator. For example, the film *Shoes Who* features close-ups of women crossing and uncrossing their legs to display the latest in footwear: **29**. An intertitle announces: 'Remember, Adam, this is a Shoe Parade' just in case men in the audience forget they are watching a fashion film. The film-makers very much enjoyed showing women in various states of undress and would use every trick in the book to film girls in their underwear. As *Eve's Film Review* was classified as news film, it did not have to be submitted for a censor's certificate. This resulted in the film-makers being able to get away with much more than they would have been able to in the feature film. However, the items of underwear usually had to have some 'novel' quality to justify lingering looks. Thus *This Freedom* begins with the intertitle: 'Nowadays, with Eve taking up all sorts of outdoor (and indoor) sports and pastimes, freedom in **dress** is essential.' Following this are shots of girls playing hockey and a woman high jumper. We then see two women trying on a new

(54)
Suits you sir –
Fashion Forecasts for Men
by Mr Leslie Henson

(55)
Freedom of dress is essential –
This Freedom

undergarment which we are told has 'No separate undie-things to work out of place – no strain on bust or waist, and it replaces the old regime in a moment'. We see shots of girls removing pieces of clothing: **55** then shadow silhouettes as they put on the new undies. The girls then do a few high kicks just to prove that freedom of movement really is possible in the new lingerie.

In many of the fashion items, close-up shots break up the body to focus on various details: **56** which can have the effect of sexualising certain parts of the anatomy or pieces of dress. This is most obvious in articles focusing on shoes or hosiery, such as *The Little Things That Matter – Stockings* where many close-ups of women's legs are justified by intertitles explaining that shapely limbs are spoiled by crooked seams. The pleasures inherent in the many *Eve's Film Review* fashion items featuring women as sexual spectacle were explored in the preceding chapter.

(56)
The broken up body –
Parisian Capes and Shapes

'Don't forget, less haste, less waist.'[6] Health and Beauty Items

Films focusing on the pursuit of beauty constitute the second largest section of *Eve's Film Review* items. Then, as now, women were encouraged by print magazines to exercise and diet to achieve a slim figure. *Eve's Film Review* took things a step further by actually showing exercise routines women could follow. Unlike television demonstrations today, women could not actually perform the exercises in front of the cinema screen so the movements had to be fairly simple. My favourite is performed by 'Olivette', a well known exhibition dancer of the day, in the charmingly titled *Shadow Shrinking Exercises – No. 2*. The routine involves placing on the floor two small bells – the type you might find on a hotel reception desk – then lying in between them on your back with arms outstretched. The aim, achieved by crossing one leg over the other whilst slightly twisting the body, is to ring the bell with one's foot! It looks very tricky, but it must have been fun for pianists accompanying the film to time a little 'ping' as Olivette's foot touched the bell. An intertitle informs the audience: 'A roll on the floor is worth two on the hips'.

The mass demonstration of exercise routines often appeared in *Eve's Film Review*, including some early footage of The Women's League of Health and Beauty: **57**. Many of these films were bought in from overseas; *Massed Misses… Of Sweden* for example shows an enormous number of women dressed in white performing a synchronised routine in a large sports stadium. As an intertitle describes it: 'The drill superb – hundreds of sweet Swedish charmers moving in synchronism'. In common with many of these items, the display is filmed from a high angle to show the patterns made by the women's bodies: **58** (we can see where Busby

Berkeley might have got some inspiration for his stupendous dance routines). An intertitle introduces the film *The New Arrivals – La Belle France Drops In*: 'The healthy athletic British girls have led the world so long in the outdoor type, that we are apt to overlook the progress made by our friends across the Channel'. After shots of a large group of French girls exercising in unison, an intertitle suggests something that we will see echoed in many of the sporting items: 'Years ago, fond Mamma in Paris would have fainted at the idea of Marie or Jeanne trying these health-giving mass exercises.'

Viewing *Eve's Film Review* items showing ways of beautifying the skin, nails, hair and body reinforces the maxim that there is 'nothing new under the sun'. Modern magazines and television programmes celebrating new trends in the twenty-first century should take a look at what was going on in the 1920s and early 30s. Designs painted on the fingernails are introduced in *Eve's Latest*

(57)
Slim and trim –
Beauty Exercises

(58)
The beauty of the
female form in motion –
Beauty Exercises

Novelty: **59**; a painted Pathe cockerel makes an appearance on a woman's shoulder in *More High Art*: **60**; and in *Permanent Tinting* a woman has rosy cheeks applied with some rather primitive tattooing equipment by a sinister man in a white coat.

Looking back on the styles of bygone eras was a favourite precursor to shots of the very latest trends. Films such as *Crowning Glories!* gave women the opportunity to model all sorts of weird and wonderful hairstyles of the past, before settling on the new permanent wave vogue. Hairdressing was big business in the 1920s. The most famous crimper of the period was Emile, whose salons were advertised in the *Tatler* as being 'the premier coiffeurs of London'. He also makes regular appearances in *Eve's Film Review*. In *Shingled – A Cutting Little Episode In One Act* we see Emile cutting very long hair into a short bob. An intertitle informs all those tentative women in the audience that 'Shingling does not injure the hair – it strengthens it and generally adds a becoming touch to

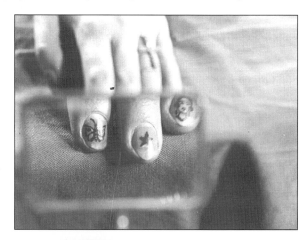

(59)
Designs painted
on fingernails –
Eve's Latest Novelty

(60)
Logo placement –
the Pathe cockerel –
More High Art

(61)
*Converting the hair
into an Eton crop –*
Hair Modes of the Moment

(62)
The Pneumakardion –
The Massage Robot

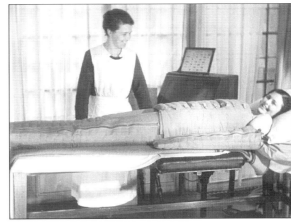

those fair ladies who decide to sacrifice tresses temporarily to fashion'. However, if you have cut your hair and then regret it, in *The Latest in Coiffures* Emile also demonstrates a style for 'Ladies just recovering from the bobbed hair vogue', which incorporates a small bun at the nape of the neck. As well as setting fashion in hairstyles, many *Eve's Film Review* items feature Emile's suggestions for hair adornments and accessories. In *Hair Modes of the Moment* some glorious bandeaux are modelled: **61,** and women are reassured that if they don't fancy the chop they can still look up to date: 'No longer need the unshingled one fear for her lovely locks. They can be converted into an almost Eton crop without losing a hair'. This is achieved by clever combing and styling of the hair and the addition of a decorative band. Emile's salons also offered beauty treatments, and several films demonstrate techniques that women could use in their own home. *Massage Tip* is a rather sensual film showing how two girlfriends can massage each others' hands, and in *Eve Dresses Her Tresses* Emile gives advice on the correct way to brush hair.

Bizarre machines and weird beauty techniques often featured in *Eve's Film Review*. The pneumakardion for example, was a padded suit into which you could be strapped to enjoy a snooze-inducing massage. An electric current made the suit contract and expand, presumably resulting in an agreeable sensation: **62**. *Eternal Youth* shows a new manipulation technique where women lie on the ground with pillows behind their heads as a female beautician holds both their legs together, vigorously swinging them from side to side. We are presented with high-angle shots of women smiling broadly from ear to ear as they are shuffled across the room with their legs swinging; it looks highly pleasurable: **63**. A strange invention known as a 'health wheel' makes a regular appearance in these films, with women strapping themselves in and wheeling themselves around with what looks like extremely dangerous and nausea-inducing speed: **64**. Outrageous (and in retrospect ridiculous) contraptions are used to remove wrinkles in *Beauty School*. Black rubber wraps are worn to correct double chins: **65** and a strap-on device is claimed to change the shape of noses. This film always provokes lots of laughter from modern audiences and presumably would have done so in the 1920s too.

(63)
Swing those hips –
Eternal Youth

(64)
Going for a spin –
The Wheel of Life

(65)
One chin or two? –
Beauty School

Many of these films poke gentle fun at women's beauty habits and attempts to fight Father Time. *To Pluck or Not to Pluck* for example investigates whether it's better to have thin eyebrows or stay hairy – 'like a monkey'. In *Beauty School* a grinding device is used to minimise wrinkles and we are told: 'Electric treatment is meted out to faces – (some deserve it, too.)' In *Women's World Today* an intertitle asks: 'And dealing with beauty, girls, how many men realise all the trouble Eve takes – mostly for "him" too – in the beauty parlours?' The secrets of female primping and preening are then revealed with shots of women having their eyelashes curled, hair permed, and faces steamed. The cinema audience is generally assumed to be as bound into beauty regimes as the women on screen. In *Yours and Theirs!* we are informed through an intertitle: 'Nobody, not even you Madam, escapes the tyranny of the powder puff.'

'It's so simple said our lady hat-maker.'[7] Educational Items

There was an edificatory impulse at work in many *Eve's Film Review* items. Perhaps the most frequent type of educational item was the dance step instruction film. Dancing was a major form of leisure activity in the 1920s, and the cinema was an ideal place to learn the latest crazes. *The French Tango, Made Easy*; *Some Steps From The Kalgoorlie Fox-Trot*; and *The Latest Dance – The Baltimore* are three of many examples which use a combination of long-shots of couples dancing and close-ups of their feet to demonstrate new dances. Some films used innovative techniques to good effect. Slow-motion filming is sometimes used to help clarify difficult steps, and in *The New Midway Rhythm Dance* an intertitle announces: 'To enable you to follow the feet more closely we give you this novel view', before a worm's eye view of the dancers' feet through a glass floor. *The New Tango* uses both this technique and a split screen effect, showing the steps as they are seen above the floor in synchronisation with the steps shot from beneath the floor.

Well known dance instructors, including Victor Silvester and Pathe's favourite Santos Casani, often appeared in these films. Santos owned 'The Largest School of Dancing in England' according to a 1928 edition of *Theatre and Film Illustrated*, and regularly appeared in *Eve's Film Review* demonstrating new dance steps. He wrote a column for the *Daily Mail* and announced himself to be 'the only teacher who has received the correct steps of the BLACK BOTTOM by telephone direct from New York'! Perhaps his performances on film helped in his success. In the film *The Flat Charleston Made Easy*, Santos and his partner José Lennard demonstrate the latest jazz dance. Cinema patrons are encouraged to 'try all these steps whilst you sit!' and the feet of the dancers are seen in close-up as they 'walk through' the steps: **66**. The film ends with a shot of the couple dancing on top of a taxi cab; an image which has since been used to represent 'the roaring twenties' in countless television documentaries: **67**.

(66)
Try these steps
whilst you sit –
The Flat Charleston
Made Easy

(67)
The Roaring Twenties –
The Flat Charleston
Made Easy

(68)
Service with the Cinema –
Dance Do's and Don'ts

> If you desire the printed details of the "Kinkajou", (with Ballroom hints) send. Postcard to
> Editor,
> Pathé's Eve's Film Review
> 103, Wardour St.,
> London, W.1.
> They will be sent free of charge,
> *"Service with the Cinema."*
>
> EVE'S FILM REVIEW

Cinema patrons were often invited to write to Pathe for free instruction leaflets explaining dance techniques. As an example of how popular these films were: for one step that Casani illustrated, 20,000 leaflets had to be printed up to cope with demand.[8] The fact that Pathe supplied these leaflets free of charge is surprising, but there is a sense that the company saw itself as having an interactive relationship with its audience, providing a service to them. This is evident in many films, including *Dance Do's and Don'ts*. After demonstrating how to hold your partner correctly and how to 'avoid ugly jerky movements caused by the man's wrong indications', Santos demonstrates a new dance – 'The Kinkajou'. An offer of free dance leaflets ends with the motto 'Service with the Cinema': **68**.

Other popular instruction films featured conjuring, recipes, and home crafts. The secrets of magic tricks were often revealed on screen (don't tell the Magic Circle) and cinema patrons were encouraged to observe and remember. 'Here's an easy trick to do when you get home …' reads an intertitle in *Tricky Tricks* and 'Here's a cute little trick to show the youngsters in an odd moment' is suggested in *Amusing The Youngsters*. Viewers are again encouraged to drop a line to Pathe in *Can You Do These?*, where after a series of close-up shots of sleight-of-hand trickery an intertitle reads: 'If you can't do it, send stamped addressed envelope to "Pathe's" 103 Wardour St. London W1 for solution.'

There are surprisingly few recipe items within *Eve's Film Review*. These were a staple feature of women's print magazines of the day but perhaps it was felt that measurements and procedures would be forgotten between the cinema and home. However, the few recipe films that exist are very cute. In *Sweets for the*

Sweet we are shown how to make Marzipan Fancies, Walnut Kisses and Stuffed Cherries. *Flake Fancies* shows how fancy biscuits are made, with this instruction to the audience: 'Now watch closely!' For the housewife there were household wisdom films including *Eve's Home Hint (A Silver Cleaning Tip)*. Cinema patrons are shown how to make tarnished silver shine like new with the aid of salt, bicarbonate of soda, a jug of hot water and a strip of zinc: **69**. A *Simple Butter Cooler* is a lovely film in which the audience is asked 'Are you troubled with this in your larder…?' before a shot of a plate of melted butter. 'It's butter … suffering from heat stroke. And here's how the housewife can prevent it…' A woman proceeds to make a nifty miniature fridge from several household items including a plant pot. The film concludes with a close-up of the woman looking very pleased with herself.

More numerous than the household tips and recipes are *Eve's* craft demonstration films. Another essential of women's print magazines of the day, home crafts was a popular subject with female audiences as several letters in the Pathe archives testify. For example, Miss L. Renahan wrote to the company from County Durham on 31st October 1928 to request pamphlets describing the

(69) Help for the housewife – Eve's Home Hint (A Silver Cleaning Tip)

(70)
Home crafts –
Festive Seasonalities

making of feather buttonholes and crystallised flowers; the process of which had been demonstrated in *Eve's Film Review* the previous week. She ends her letter as follows: 'I need hardly say how much I enjoy your *Eve's Film Reviews*, they are so educational and easy to follow it is quite a pleasure to watch them, and they end only too soon.'

The many craft demonstration films within the series include *Introducing Miss Tea Cosy* (how to make a tea cosy from a broken doll and some fabric), *The Latest – Fishbone Flowers!* (making brooches from fishbones!), and *Why Not This Crepe Paper Hat For Summer?* (natty headgear made from plaited strips of crepe paper). Making lovely things for the home is sometimes shown as a pastime for mothers and daughters to enjoy together. In *Festive Seasonalities* a little girl helps her mother to make Christmas decorations and gifts: **70**, and *The Bead Makers* shows a woman and young girl making a bead curtain. The latter film is also a good example of the recurring theme of thriftiness in these craft items; the beads are made from old posters which the mother and daughter have cut up. In *Odds and Ends* an intertitle proclaims: 'Anti-waste! – Politicians preach it, but mother knows best how to practise it. A gingham remnant – a little daughter who always needs a new pinafore – suggest a lightning "Anti-waste" campaign to Eve's inventive mind'. In *Solving a Slippery Problem* a pair of dancing shoes is transformed into a comfy pair of slippers. A satisfied intertitle proclaims: 'And there you are – and enough money saved to take you to the pictures every day for a week!'

Adam sometimes makes his presence felt in these craft films, but always offscreen. In *Running The Gauntlet* the processes involved in making a pair of fabulous leather gloves are shown. Women are encouraged: 'If Adam's away, his razor cuts quite nicely – but don't tell him we told you!' In *A Photo Novelty for Eve* an intertitle suggests: 'If Eve isn't handy with a small saw or chisel, get hubby (or one of the boy friends) to help'. But in general it is the resourcefulness and the capability of women to create beautiful things to wear or decorations for the home that is celebrated in these films. The theme running throughout is that the creativeness of women knows no bounds.

'Buxom wenches, and equally at home with oxen or crops'.[9] Work Items

In the 1920s popular feature films presented a lifestyle out of reach for most cinemagoers. Many films (especially British productions) were set in the world of high society; a land of champagne, designer fashions and unlimited leisure time. Sometimes female cinemagoers would be presented with working class heroines to whom they might feel more able to relate. These heroines usually followed a Cinderella trajectory, starting their journey as a shop girl or secretary then marrying the boss or becoming a film star.[10]

Eve's Film Review offered a more down-to-earth view of women's lives. Women were given the chance to see on screen contemporaries very much like themselves – ordinary women doing ordinary jobs and enjoying ordinary hobbies. Women at work were often featured, sometimes to illustrate the particular steps involved in a manufacturing process. *Dunlop Sports Shoes – Watch Them Made At Liverpool* shows the part each of a large number of women has in making tennis shoes; *A Sweet Fragment From The 'Dessert' Island* illustrates jam making techniques in Tasmania; and *Just Buttons* shows large numbers of women and young girls at work in a button factory. There are numerous strangely pleasing films of women doing apparently simple jobs, such as *In Daffodil Land* in which women in Spalding cut, sort and bundle the Daffodil harvest: **71**. *Hollywood in Herts* shows women collecting holly, and *Eve and the Orange Harvest* pictures 'Nimble fingers wrapping up each morsel of fruit for the hungry packing cases'.

An increasing number of British women had begun going out to work during the First World War, and then continued to do so in the 1920s; especially young single women. Although most women were employed in domestic service, textile and dress manufacture, and shop and office work, an inspirational number of women are featured in *Eve's Film Review* doing unusual and surprising jobs.[11] Titles and intertitles combine to suggest that the world is Eve's oyster – she can be anything she desires to be. In *More Jobs! Quaint and Queer* we meet a woman meteorologist and a female elephant trainer; *Eve – Editor, Publisher, Seller* features a one-woman newspaper producer; *Nerve!* presents a female lion tamer; and *Odd Jobs for Eve* include firewoman and aviatrix. In *The Village Smithy Stands*, two female blacksmiths demonstrate their prowess. In a shot at the end showing the two women posing outside the smithy, they look shy and embarrassed about being filmed: **72**. A truly remarkable film, *Women Private Investigators* shows women learning how to disguise themselves as men, handle obstreperous shoplifters, restrain crooks and 'shadow' suspects. The

(71)
Eve at work –
In Daffodil Land

(72)
Coyness is nice –
The Village Smithy Stands

location of this story? Baker Street, naturally.

After showing the audience examples of women with extraordinary jobs, the denouement of the film *Odd Jobs for Eve* is introduced by an intertitle: 'But after all is said and done, woman's noblest job of all is —' followed by shots of a woman and her 13 children. This is very unusual amongst the *Eve's Film Review* items featuring women who have a career, possibly because the film is an American item retitled for the British market. Most of the films showing working women do not compare the life of the career girl with the more traditional role of wife and mother. Generally, women who work and women who bring up children are equally, but separately, respected within *Eve's Film Review*.

The makers of these films acknowledged the fact that many of the women watching the cinemagazine would have had children and the role of wife and mother was celebrated, although not to the same extent as other occupations.

(73)
*Every mother can
relate to this –*
The Annual Howlfeast

(74)
Washing day –
Going to the Dogs

(75)
Cuteness –
Furry Little Ones –
Something for the Kiddies

94

Due to the loss of life during the First World War women were being encouraged by some government departments to have children, and *Eve's Film Review* often featured toddlers in a manner designed to provoke murmurs of recognition amongst the female public. Modern day screenings always result in a ripple of appreciative comments at the sight of cute babies and children and presumably would have done so at the time they were originally shown. Baby shows were a regular subject for *Eve's Film Review*. Intertitles such as 'There's one thing this tough old world will never tire of – a cuddle. And the friendliest piece of cuddle is – Baby!' introduce shots of cute babies being fussed over by their mothers.[12] That women in the audience would understand and relate to the trials and tribulations of motherhood is often acknowledged within these films. An item called *The Annual Howlfeast* features a baby competition where most of the contestants seem to be crying – it is odd that seeing lots of babies crying should cause amusement but it undoubtedly does – an intertitle referring to the bawling reads: 'It doesn't need a "talkie" to speak this language – every mother knows it': **73**. Gentle fun is poked at the tendency for parents to consider their child to be the centre of the universe by referring to children as 'His (or Her) Majesty the Baby'. Many films feature the latest in prams or high chairs for babies or toys for toddlers, and a few show new fashions for children. That women (and the children who might accompany them to the cinema) would enjoy films of animals is also apparent within *Eve's Film Review* with numerous stories featuring dogs, cats, rabbits and other cute creatures. The cameraman was definitely on to a winner if he could put together stories which featured children *and* animals, such as: *Going to the Dogs*: **74** ; or even better, children *as* animals: **75**.

That women in the audience could be holding down a job as well as caring for children is sometimes acknowledged within *Eve's Film Review*. Films such as *Taking Care of Tiny Tots* and *Children of the Day* showed what children got up to in their day nurseries whilst their mothers were out at work, and *A Super Nursery* shows 'the most modern mother and baby nursery in the world' in Manneheim, Germany. That motherhood is not always rosy is touchingly illustrated in *A Leaf From Life,* where mothers leave their children at a hospital for tuberculosis treatment then collect them in the evening. Working mothers who feature in *Eve's Film Review* are often those who have succeeded in the arts world. Thus artists such as Mrs E. Macavity and Mabel Lucie Attwell are both presented as loving mothers. Actresses or stage performers often get the chance to show off their offspring to the camera. These include Virginia Moore-Duprez joining her mother May in a clog dance, and toddler Joan Dorian performing some ballet steps with her mother Kathleen.[13]

Many young girls who visited the cinema would become mothers themselves, a fact that is acknowledged in films such as *Little Mothers At The Lawn Lane L.C.C. Girls' School*, where preteen girls are taught in 'mothercraft' classes how to change nappies and the correct way to hold and bathe babies. This type of film however is outweighed by those showing young female cinemagoers the other job options which might be open to them. *Land Students in Training* shows young women at their studies at Swanley Horticultural College; in *Eve at College – A Harrogate Study* young students are shown learning art and chemistry; and in *Nautical Naughties* girls learn how to be sailors.

'They're love-like, And dove-like, They're Angels from above-like'[14]
Leisure and Holiday Items

Due to the loss of male life during the First World War there was a distinct shortage of men to go around during the 1920s. Many working single girls had money to spend on leisure activities, and there are numerous *Eve's Film Review* items showing women on holiday together or spending time partaking in 'all-girls' activities.

Perhaps the nicest of the holiday items is *No-Man's Land*. This three and a half minute film features women of the Queen Mary's Army Auxiliary Corps renewing old friendships at a Thames island holiday camp. The women spend time swimming, cooking, larking around, smoking, and listening to a gramophone: **76**. The general impression is that they are enjoying themselves immensely in their 'Adamless Eden' and as is common with this kind of item, when the girls make up their beds for the night an intertitle reads: 'That's quite sufficient Mr. Cameraman, Goodnight'. We see in *Eve All At Sea* girls having fun on a pleasure liner in the Mediterranean, and in *Her Royal Ski Ness* girls lark around at a ski resort; sledging, throwing snowballs and posing for the cameraman: **77**.

Seaside locations were popular spots for the Pathe cameramen to capture images of bathing belles and girls having fun together. *The Day in Deauville* features many shots of women posing in their swimsuits and a woman performing body building exercises on the sand. *Beach Pebbles* begins with the intertitle: 'Some of the prettiest pebbles we know lie about the beach at Deauville' and includes footage of women sunbathing, paddling in the sea, and exercising. In an effort to capture as many women in swimsuits as possible the Pathe cameramen also frequented swimming pools and lidos to film girls having fun. *Buoyant Belles – at Droitwich Spa* shows chorus girls modelling swim-wear, then floating on their backs in the water. As the baths are filled with medicinal brine water, everything is buoyant and the girls help themselves to cups of tea and biscuits from a table which floats in the pool. In the film *Water Witches* a shot of a large number of girls posing around a fountain is preceded by an intertitle: 'This picture explains why Adam frequents the pools so eagerly – because of the water witches there'.[15] This is followed by shots of girls sitting on the edge of the Hornsey open air swimming pool splashing with their feet, and general high jinx in and around the water.

(76)
An Adamless Eden –
No-Man's Land

(77)
Ski larks –
Her Royal Ski Ness

(78)
Pulchritude –
We Go to Coventry! –
And the Reason Why

An interesting variation on the 'girls having fun' theme can be seen in *We Go to Coventry! – And the Reason Why* where we are introduced to a group of less than svelte swimmers who are apparently the 'largest married Ladies Swimming Section in Britain'. They are definitely not your typical bathing belles but they are having just as much fun. An intertitle informs us that they are 'All married ladies and able to hold their own anywhere!' Their displays of swimming strokes, lifesaving techniques and general water baby antics are followed by an end sequence of the women smiling and laughing: **78**. Films of women having fun together often end with an 'emblematic shot' of the girls smiling at the camera and by implication at the cinema audience.

Camping and caravanning are shown to be ideal amusements for a group of girls. Two films which share the title *Where My Caravan Is Rested* feature wonderful fold-out caravans. The first film has two girls towing their 'covered wagon' to a beauty spot, then jumping out of the car to open it out. The girls smile and laugh throughout as does the group of four friends in the other film of the same title. When they arrive at their chosen location they spring out of the car with lots of 'pep', taking deep breaths of country air and throwing their arms about in excitement at being on holiday. An intertitle reads: 'The only item missing is – ? (Guess it, Adam!);' but we can see that the girls are having a great time without men as they dance together in the open air to music from their wind-up gramophone: **79**.

Gangs of girls are often seen enjoying each others' company on days out as well as longer holidays. A popular film subject for the *Eve's Film Review* cameraman was the funfair. Kinetic activity abounds and shots are often taken from inside fairground rides. Girls are seen screaming with laughter on a 'cups and saucer

(79)
Who misses Adam? –
Where My Caravan
Is Rested

98

ride' in *Kursaal Southend* and having fun in motorised boats in *Hey Ho! Come to the Fun Fair!* Favourite scenarios for cameramen at funfairs are those in which women inadvertently expose their knickers. Helter Skelter rides are particularly good for this, as cameramen wait at the bottom for girls to come straight at them (in *Fair's Fair!* for example). In *Shies and Shes* a sequence showing a girl reaching the bottom of the Helter Skelter with her skirt around her waist looks suspiciously posed, unlike in *Fairs for the Fair* where girls hang on to their skirts in a vain attempt to preserve their dignity. They laugh while they are doing it though!

'A run on the field is worth two in the stocking'.[16] Sports Items

Sporty girls were big news in the 1920s. Articles in newspapers posed questions about whether jumping around on the sports field was detrimental to women's reproductive organs, and *Eve's Film Review* echoed these concerns with film titles such as: *Is Cricket a Suitable Game for Eve?*; *Is Eve Going Too Far In Athletics?*; and *Should Girls Box?* Despite their questioning titles, the impression given in these, and all the sporty *Eve* films, is that women are more than capable of succeeding in any sport they try.

Films featuring sportswomen often contrasted the graceful, elegant Eve of yesteryear with her lithe and agile modern counterpart. In *Peace and Pace* an intertitle remarks: 'It seems only yesterday that Eve was content to form part of a peaceful background' before shots of women relaxing on a bed of cushions, shielding themselves from the sun with parasols as their punt is propelled along a river. Another intertitle observes: 'Today she leads the speedy sporting life – in the Rugger fields of France.' The river scene is contrasted with a rough and tumble French women's rugby game. In *Flying Legs – Filmed at Gravesend* we are told: 'Grandmamma would need her smelling salts still more to get over the shock if she could only see the hard-running sporting Eve of today', before shots of an athletics meet for women: 'Girls never ran like this in *her* day, poor dear!' In *Lady Wrestlers* we are told 'A few years ago the idea of a girl in "shorts" for running was enough to make Grandma gasp, but these Eves believe a "bout" a day keeps the Doctor away.'

Are Women's Sports Too Strenuous? is a perfect example of how the power of these images of sportswomen transcends any negative framework imposed on them through titles and intertitles. The film begins with an intertitle: 'Gone are the days when Eve figured as a slow-moving kind of frieze – (and froze!)'. Women dressed in Greek tunics walk hand in hand on a cliff top, then perform a stylised dance: **80**. This elegance is contrasted with women on the sports field. 'Today Eve is outstripping Adam in more senses than one' we are told, and there then follows a cavalcade of images of sporty girls. Shots of a women's cross country running event, a sprinting race, two crazy female motorcyclists: **81**, a discus

(80)
Graceful Eves –
Are Women's Sports Too
Strenuous?

(81)
Modern Eves –
Are Women's Sports Too
Strenuous?

thrower and a long-jumper flash past the viewer. After this impressive display of feminine prowess an intertitle reads, 'But, somewhere in this wide world they still seek gracefulness'. This is followed by a final shot of the elegant dancers seen earlier, continuing their open air cavorting. When screened for modern audiences, this last shot always provokes laughter from women. The power of the sporty women is *not* undercut by the intertitle and final shot. If this was the intention of the filmmakers (and I don't think it really was), it fails. What we remember are images of lots of women enjoying their sport, and other women enjoying dancing on a cliff top – each to their own!

The 'get up and go' of the sporty girl is celebrated in these films, and in an item called *Pep!* we are informed that pep is: 'That piquant, pert but descriptive word that describes so eloquently in one syllable the energy of modern Eve'. Many of the sports items do not feature famous sportswomen, they are more often ordinary women who have taken up sport in their leisure time. Films such as

Fighting Father Time feature sports day for the 'Nippies' – Lyons Corner House waitresses, and in *Girls of the Wheel Brigade* Nippies are seen whizzing round the cycle track at Herne Hill. Other items demonstrate how young women are participating in sports at school or college. *Lacrosse Leaps* shows students at Queen Alexandra's House P.T. College learning the basics; *M'Lady of the Foil* sees a group of young women fencers, and *The Baseball Belles From Cardiff* features Welsh schoolgirls in gymslips attempting the American national game. Occasionally the sports items offer an opportunity for a glimpse of stocking or underwear and many celebrate the beauty of the female form with slow motion footage of diving, running, and swimming. *Sportists* offers a particularly nice example of 'cheesecake' footage, with shots of five women archers wearing nothing more than bathing suits, engaged in target practice in a snow covered woodland: **82**. Often the sports items celebrate the camaraderie to be had from team games, with lovely shots of girls with their arms around each other after a strenuous game of football: **83**, or posing with friends for team shots: **84**.

(82)
Brr! –
Sportists

(83)
Buddies –
Playing Adam's Game

Whether it be darts, wrestling, boxing, cricket, rowing, fencing, athletics or any number of sporting activities, *Eve's Film Review* is proof of the fact that in the 1920s and 30s women were doing it all. As an intertitle in *The Rival Sex* ruefully observes: 'No sport is safe from her restless feet – not even football!'

'Truly feminine – and attractive – in spite of her strenuous flying'[17]
Items Featuring Extraordinary Women

Cinemagoers of the 1920s and 1930s often found themselves in the company of cowgirls, women aviators, stunt drivers, martial arts experts, lion tamers, and motor racers. Women with a penchant for dangerous sports and hair-raising antics often made an appearance in the weekly women's film. Hair raising spins around the racetrack at Brooklands and vertigo-inducing aircraft wing-walking stunts gave women, from the safety of their cinema seats, a taste of the freedom experienced by some of their contemporaries. There is a strong sense of liberation in many of these films, a feeling that these women believed that anything was possible. By its very nature as a cinemagazine, *Eve's Film Review* is a rich mosaic of images of women in a cornucopian variety of pastimes, occupations, and states of pleasure.

Women aviators were big news throughout the 1920s and 1930s. Amelia Earhart, Jean Batten, and Britain's own Amy Johnson were regularly the subject of newsreel stories, and *Eve's Film Review* featured longer portraits of women with wings. Many of these films do not name the inspirational women we see, and there is often a sequence shot to prove that women who take to the skies are still feminine despite their bravery. In *Air Thrills for Eve* for example, a woman who stands on the top wing of a biplane while it 'loops the loop' is seen on terra firma later touching up her makeup. Accompanying the shots of Maryse Bastie, the holder of the Women's World Endurance Flight Record: **85** is an intertitle describing her as being 'truly feminine – and attractive – in spite of her strenuous flying'. But there is still respect for these 'women with wings'. The beautifully shot and edited film *A Really New Occupation for Eve* proudly announces that 'In Britain there are only 3 holders of the "B" Flying License, which permits a Pilot to take paying passengers – Miss Pauline Gower is one of them'.[18]

Speed became an issue of national importance in the 1920s. Many records were being broken by trains and boats and planes, and women wanted to get in on the act too. Women motor boat racers such as Joe Carstairs wanted to compete on the same terms as men, and 'the weaker sex' set out to prove that anything men could do they could do better. *Eve's Film Review* rejoiced in the speed with which women racing drivers roared around a race track, and *Sporting Eves – Miss Ivy Cummins*

(84)
Friendship through sport –
Eve in Training

(85)
Attractive and feminine –
Camera Interviews –
Mlle Marise Daspie (sic)
[actually, Maryse Bastie]

(86)
Deeply interested in bonnets –
Camera Interviews –
Miss Ivy Cummins
The Racing Motorist

(87)
Sailing the seven seas –
Sailor Girl

(88)
Not bad for a girl –
The Rival

The Racing Motorist showed Ivy accompanied by her mechanic (who also happens to be her mother) having a great time at Brooklands with not a man in sight: **86**. As Ivy inspects her sparkplugs a title observes that she – like most Eves – is 'deeply interested in a bonnet…'

Other women who are seen attempting feats more usually associated with men include Joan Lowell, an eccentric tobacco chewing woman who has 'sailed the seven seas'. We see her enthusiastically climbing ropes aboard ship, then spitting over her shoulder as she pretends to sail her obviously stationary vessel through rough weather: **87**.[19] *The Rival* shows a Texas cowgirl 'whose skill with a rope rivals her brothers'' performing tricks with a lasso on the range. A begrudgingly appreciative title prompts admiration for her skills: 'How's this – for a girl?' and the film ends with a 'glamour shot' of the cowgirl posing with her horse: **88**. Courageous women who desire to swim the channel include Ivy Hawke and Miss Doris Hines who are 'anxious to show how Eve can get along without a buoy.'[20] Another feisty lady featured is Ida Kathrena, the holder of the record for persistent bashing of a punch ball (the type of device used by boxers to practice their technique): **89**. In a hilarious film entitled *Another Record-Breaker* we see Ida keeping the ball moving whilst still managing to drink a cup of tea, eat a biscuit, smoke a cigarette and apply some face powder.

Many of the wild and outrageous ladies who fall into our category of 'extraordinary women' were entertainers. *The Leaper* shows a pretty impressive driving stunt involving a very glamorous unnamed woman driver. *Walking the Wire* features a woman doing high kicks on a tightrope; *Very Run-Down* sees a stunt woman run over by several cars, and 'Miss McGunnis' performs daredevil horse riding feats in *The Trick Rider*.[21] Two truly remarkable women also worthy of mention are Resista and Thelmina. The former displays her talent of 'changing her weight at will' in *The Light Lady Heavyweight*. Strongman Thomas Inch finds he cannot lift her when she wills her weight to increase from seven stones to forty stones before our very eyes! *Thelmina the Electric Woman* has an equally astounding

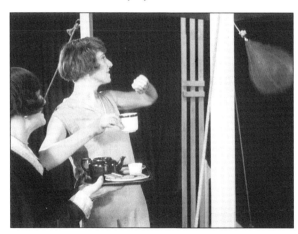

(89)
Ida Kathrena –
Another Record-Breaker

(90)
Electrifying! –
Thelmina the Electric
Woman

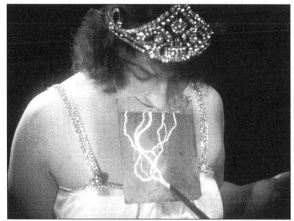

talent: **90**. She makes an electric current with her body that enables her to illuminate light bulbs, light cigarettes, and set fire to a piece of paper with the heel of her shoe.

Often the remarkable skills of women are accompanied by sequences presumably designed to show that they are, after all, women like any others. 'Jeanne' who is claimed to be 'the strongest woman in the world' applies makeup before lifting weights, and Resista is seen scoffing a box of chocolates awarded to her by the defeated Thomas Inch. However, an intertitle serves to suggest that she deserves them: 'After this demonstration (witnessed by many Press Representatives) who says "the weaker sex"?' It seems to me that the sheer volume of inspirational images of women stunt drivers, aviators, sailors and cowgirls vastly outweighs attempts to belittle their efforts by the addition of jokey intertitles or 'feminising' shots. After all, why shouldn't a female body builder wear lipstick?

Artistic women were sometimes featured in *Eve's Film Review* and it is clear that these women were also held in high esteem. An intertitle in a film featuring painter Laura Knight observes that she is only the second woman to be elected an Associate of the Royal Academy since the eighteenth century. We see Ms Knight at work and a selection of her paintings is shown: **91**. Another artist featured is the sculptress Phoebe Stabler. An intertitle informs us that she was 'the designer of the famous World's Land-Speed Trophy (held by the late Sir Henry Segrave) one of her most beautiful creations.'[22] Films focusing on women highly thought of in their field eschew the usual humorous titles. A sense of the film-makers' admiration for these women is apparent through the care that has been taken with lighting, framing and editing.

(91)
A respected artist –
Camera Interviews –
Mrs Laura Knight

(92)
The Woman in Bronze –
Producing a Cabaret Show

'And so to bed – it's dawn!'[23] **Nightlife and Theatrical Entertainment Items**
During the mid 1920s there was an explosion of nightclubs and venues offering entertainment with supper. The trend seems to have been for the wealthy to go to a theatre performance then on to a club or cabaret venue for food, late night drinking, dancing and entertainment. Many of the clubs were exclusive 'members only' establishments or so popular that you had to be recognised by the doorman to gain entry. For those who could never hope to actually experience the hottest spots in town, *Eve's Film Review* offered a peep inside through its nightlife items.

Perhaps the most glamorous of the clubs of the 1920s was the Kit Cat Club. Located on the Haymarket in London, it was the favourite late night fun spot of film stars, composers, writers, and singers. In the first of a series of films featuring night spots, *Famous Clubs And Cabarets No 1. The Kit Cat Club*, Pathe caught on film many bright young things enjoying the atmosphere, smoking and drinking and taking a turn on the dance floor. An intertitle poses a challenge to the audience: 'And here's a constellation of "Stars" – see if you can "spot" them. Sophie Tucker, Gladys Cooper, Jack Hilton, George Grossmith, Tallulah Bankhead, "Delysia", Fay Marbe, Ethel Levey, Lew Hearn, Cissie Loftus, Heather Thatcher, Ella Retford, Estelle Brodie, Peggy O'Neil & Irving Berlin!' The camera pans across the group of chatting personalities as we try to put names to faces. Other 'Famous Clubs and Cabarets' captured on film by Pathe include the Piccadilly Hotel, the Metropole, Murray's Club, the Trocadero, and the Cosmo Club.

The films in this series are a valuable record not just of the style of dress and dancing of the time, but also of the cabaret acts that were offered as entertainment. A number of acts were filmed *in situ* at the club and include such

107

(93)
Muriel or Mildred Melrose –
The Real "Black Bottom"
Dance

(94)
Androgyny in action –
Clothes and the Woman

(95)
Face fungus –
At Home with Harry Tate

performers as Barrie Oliver (known as The Charleston King), the hilarious Hank the Mule (two men in a pantomime horse costume) and the Woman in Bronze who danced around tables at the Grafton Gallery holding a smoking pot: **92**.[24] In addition to filming acts as they were performed on the cabaret circuit, Pathe invited many performers to the studio on the top floor of their Wardour Street office.[25] There a whole routine was recorded in front of a backdrop – usually curtains with a few strategically placed pot plants. Many exhibition dances were filmed, such as *Tiptoe Dancers*, which features Dick Barstow dancing on a piano in ballet shoes then jumping off and landing on his toes. Mildred Melrose[26] does a mean shimmy in *The Real "Black Bottom" Dance*: **93,** and a beefy Aston flings his partner Xenia around the stage in a marvellous 'Apache' style display of acrobatics and machismo in *Terpsichore*. The duo represent strength and grace respectively and the sexual nature of their passionate dance is clear: **48**. The performance ends with Aston throwing an exhausted Xenia down on a couch and walking off; as she lies there the camera moves in towards her comatose body and her arm falls towards the floor – she is dead!

Unless comedians had a non-verbal routine they were not generally filmed for *Eve's Film Review* due to the limitations of the reel being silent. An amusing exception to this rule is stand-up Con Ingham telling a joke in *Are You a Lip-Reader?* The audience has to try to follow his exaggerated mouth movements and facial contortions. Most filmed comic routines however were of the slapstick nature, such as that performed by two clowns who blow smoke at each other in *Camera Interviews – The Arnaut Brothers The Famous Musical Clowns;* or visual jokes such as Chaz eating cigarettes and part of his shirt front in *Eccentricity*.[27] Hetty King gets a chance to show her famous male impersonations in *Clothes and the Woman* as she takes on the personas of a toff, an east-ender and a cowboy. Dissolves and a split-screen technique are used to show Hetty off to full advantage: **94**.

A popular strand of films within *Eve's Film Review* which gave audiences a chance to see their favourite personalities was the 'At Home With…' series. Stars were usually seen at their homes or in their gardens, giving them a chance to fool around for the camera without having to perform a particular sketch. Thus we have film of Harry Tate, both with and without his famous 'face fungus': **95**; Billy Merson showing off his riverside home; and Nellie Wallace enjoying a funny novel with her sister. Stage and screen personalities were also featured in this type of film; Gertrude Lawrence pulls faces in *Off Stage Moments* and Lorna and Toots Pounds, Madge Saunders, Leslie Henson, and Evelyn Laye can be seen in 'The Stars as They Are' series.[28] Films such as *After the Play is Over* give the impression that theatre and film personalities live in each others' pockets as we see Ruby Miller, Leslie Henson, Madge Saunders, Dorothy Dickson, Dorothy

Minto, Fred Allandale, Gertrude Lawrence, Cathleen Nesbitt, Sybil Thorndike, and Billy Leonard all having fun together in the same nightclub: **96**.

The late night cabaret venues all had their dancing girls as did the larger theatrical revue shows. There were the Athos Beauties from the New Princes Cabaret, the Chelsea Follies, Charlot's Girls and perhaps most famously Mr Cochran's Young Ladies. Pathe loved all dancing girls and there are many, many films featuring chorus lines. The most straightforward of these items record actual routines in stage shows. Thus we see chorus girls in gymslips, fur trimmed ice-skating outfits and nothing much more than fig leaves.[29] Particularly favoured were routines which exposed undergarments, such as the girls flashing their bloomers in *A Peep At 'Playtime At The Piccadilly Cabaret' – London*: **97**. In

(96)
Stars have fun –
After the Play is Over

(97)
Bloomers –
A Peep At Playtime At The
Piccadilly Cabaret – London

(98)
No wrinkled stockings –
Here and There

Here and There Archie De Bear's Chelsea Follies are seen performing a routine which involves seductively pulling to one side their split skirts and smoothing wrinkles out of their stockings: **98**. Typically, a low camera angle is used when filming this kind of dancing. This serves to show the maximum amount of leg on screen and also, on occasion, a glimpse of stocking top.

Films of auditions and rehearsals for stage shows also gave an opportunity to see dancing girls in action. In *Those Rehearsals* we are informed that 'Every dance has to be explained in detail and practised until those shapely limbs have just the right amount of pep and snappiness', as girls rehearse for the show 'Belle of New York'. In *Dance Factory* some extremely high kicks follow the intertitle: 'Only loose limbs will enable a girl to attain this "high art"', and in *Footwork Fancy* girls put themselves through all sorts of painful looking contortions as they limber up for a show. *The Evolution of a Show Girl* is an amusing depiction of the selection process for the chorus line of a Cochran show. Cochran, a theatrical impresario who staged musicals, revues and cabaret shows throughout England actually appears in the film (he was famously camera shy). It begins with the intertitle: 'Footlights! Every girl in the world as some time or another has imagined herself looking over them at a spellbound audience. But, before any girl can get on the stage, she must meet with some Manager's approval.' There follows an animated depiction of the casting couch at work (applicants have to sit on the Manager's lap for a cuddle), then real footage of an audition. We see the chosen girls rehearsing a routine in their practice clothes, then in flamboyant costumes demonstrating the same routine on stage: **99**.

Chorines were probably the favourite subject of the *Eve's Film Review* cameramen. Natural born performers, they were even better than fashion mannequins for acting up to the camera. Thus we see them in all sorts of bizarre situations and locations. Sometimes the name of the show they are in is mentioned, so perhaps the films served as publicity. More often we are not told who they are, they simply appear as something nice to look at on screen. Thus *Snowy Showy Girls* features a group of girls dancing in the snow in their bathing suits, and in *Spring Has Come* scantily clad girls help to give an elephant a bath. *Shivers!* includes a shot of a girl in a swimsuit sitting on a block of ice: **100**, and in *Giving the Miss to Miss Adipose* we see a high kick routine by the sea: **101**. There

(99)
Results of the casting couch –
The Evolution of a Show
Girl

(100)
Catch! –
Shivers

112

(101)
High Kicks –
Giving the Miss to
Miss Adipose

(102)
Surprise! –
The Rivals –
Some Chippings From the
New Splinters Dancing
Troupe

is little justification for most of these films apart from the pleasure gained from seeing pretty girls on screen. There are often jokey references to how Pathe cameramen struggled to keep their minds on the job. In the film *Illusions* for example, footage of a bevy of beauties is preceded by the intertitle: 'lots of muscular effort was needed to keep our Cameraman's eyes from wandering when he "shot" these – !'

The nightlife and entertainment items within *Eve's Film Review* are the only items in which men regularly appear, while the others focus almost entirely on women. In what is possibly the funniest of all *Eve's Film Review* items, a traditional dance routine turns into something different when the girls in the chorus line retire backstage. The seven high kicking chicks fling themselves into chairs, light cigarettes and drink beer. Suddenly taking off their wigs they reveal their true identity – men! An intertitle reads: 'Conclusive proof that 'men were deceivers ever' isn't it girls?': **102**.

7 – An Adamless Eden

Around the time that *Eve's Film Review* was released the following paragraph appeared in the gossip column of *The Film Renter and Moving Picture News*:

'Since Pathe have announced the institution of the first women's film, *'Eve's Film Review'*, they have received numerous requests for the production of a film for men. Hints on how to avoid the Income Tax collector and convince the wife that one has been kept late at the office are amongst the suggestions for suitable contents.'[1]

The suggestions for a cinemagazine directed specifically at a male audience are obviously somewhat tongue in cheek. However, it is true to say that at the time *Eve's Film Review* was on cinema screens in Britain the interests and pleasures of men and women were culturally defined as being different. The belief that films about fashion and beauty would appeal to 'the innate Eve in [all] women' was held by the makers and critics of *Eve's Film Review*. Conversely, in society at large in the 1920s and 1930s for a man to actively acknowledge enjoyment of these things would have seemed unusual unless he was involved in a professional capacity, as an haute couture designer or hairdresser for example. A curiosity about 'women's things' might be tolerated, but a man actively involved in traditionally 'feminine' domains would be subject to suggestions of effeminacy. However, although men and women were *supposed* to enjoy different pleasures at this time it would be patently false to suggest that *all* women were interested in fashion and no (real) men were. Within the cinema, the sexual identity of the viewer becomes blurred. Seated in the dark the spectator is invited to stare at the screen and can enjoy the images without having to justify the appropriateness of his or her pleasure. The female body, the frocks and the frou-frou fripperies of the feminine wardrobe are on display for both men and women in *Eve's Film Review*. For those of us who do appreciate these pleasures, the films are a pure delight.

Eve's Film Review is a hugely enjoyable collection of films made *for* women and *about* women. If they were made *by* women I wonder if they would have been dramatically different; it is impossible to say. I agree with Wendy Lesser's statement however that 'The rich world of men's artistic visions of women cannot be summarized with a mere reference to the artists' sex.'[2] The men who made *Eve's Film Review* were making films that they thought women would enjoy, with one eye on making them entertaining for men too. The fact remains that the films are full to bursting with fabulous footage of women's pleasures and acheivements. In the 'Adamless Eden' of *Eve's Film Review* we are given a revealing and inspirational glimpse into the lives of women during the 1920s and early 1930s, even if it is seen through the eyes of men.

My intention in this book has been to celebrate the existence of this collection of films. It is remarkable that so many of them have survived at Pathe and in other archives around the world. Some seventy-odd years after they were made, the films still have the power to entertain, charm, amaze and inform. By virtue of longevity of the series and extremely wide range of subject matter of the films, it seems to me that they are valuable documents; not only for the film student but also for social historians, particularly those interested in women's history. I hope that in suggesting some of the ways these films can be 'read' this study might stimulate academic and possibly commercial interest in the collection. It has always been my belief that *Eve's Film Review* should be shared with audiences through public screenings. Now, through the internet, it is becoming possible for even more people to see the films.

I know that modern audiences enjoy *Eve's Film Review*. I only wish I had more testimony from cinemagoers who saw the films in the 1920s and 1930s. Contemporary commendations have been almost impossible to find, but I'll end this chapter with two. The first demonstrates that those who enjoyed the films would have been in good company. In *The Film Renter and Moving Picture News* of December 2nd 1922 a grand claim was made:

'It may be of interest to our readers to know that the highest in the land, our beloved Queen, has shown special interest in these films, and was particularly pleased with the Slow Motion pictures. In fact, we may safely say that the weekly editions of the *Pathé Pictorial* and *Eve and Everybody's Film Review* hold an unrivalled position in the hearts of the British people wherever domiciled.'[3]

The last word however goes to Phyllis Chambers who wrote a letter to Pathe on the 13th October 1928. She suggested that a Pathe film of people walking along muddy streets in different ways would prove illuminating, 'so that we could all then adopt the clean way and save our silk stockings!' The ending of this letter seems to suggest that *Eve's Film Review* was indeed seen by some women as 'a friend and advisor in the difficult task of being a woman', as well as a space where women's pleasures and achievements could be celebrated. The letter certainly gives an idea of how women might 'use' *Eve's Film Review* to explore issues of importance to them, however frivolous they might seem to others and whatever the attitude of the male film-makers. Miss Chambers' letter concludes:

'Of course I am writing merely as a "picture-goer" and know nothing of the technical side and whether this would be practicable – but I thought I would just give you my idea on how you could be very useful to my sister "Eves"!'

Appendix 1

JUST "PIC and EVE" – By EDITOR WATTS

The PATHE PICTORIAL has now filled an important niche in the structure of the perfect programme for over 11 years and every year increases its prestige as the World's most popular and varied "Interest" film.

The keynote of the PICTORIAL'S progress is personified in its slogans -
"Puts the World before You."
"To See Much is to Learn Much".

Yet the PICTORIAL does not attempt to enforce education upon an audience.

We realise our primary business is to entertain, amuse and interest our audiences – though, if at the same time anyone wishes to learn anything new from the pictures (and all of us are able to) he or she is very welcome.

The store from which we gather our subjects, is the world, and we search the world for our material. Very few spots on the globe are not visited at one time or another by the ubiquitous "PIC" Cameraman, or our Agents, whether on top of the highest mountain or deep below the sea.

The latest scientific inventions and novelties figure in our contents. Even the marvellous evolution of the cinema itself, from its early days up to today is being successfully exploited in a series of fascinating "Evolution" subjects in the PICTORIAL.

Films, twenty, thirty years and even older have been unearthed by us and are being shown to the public in interesting and amusing instalments, and these items bid fair to be even more popular, as we have just obtained many more.

Incidentally, these attractive items are being included in the ordinary way, and showmen need not book some of the present "Yesterday and Today" films being offered at fancy prices by other people.

Tales of adventure, expeditions, interviews with notable people, coloured films, those wonderful flower subjects (about which we have had many letters), daring stunts, queer corners and industries of the world, camera novelties and tricks, fascinating nature studies, unique slow-motion films, sporting and scientific items, all these are covered by the PICTORIAL in its search for the ever new and interesting.

No effort is spared to keep the PICTORIAL in the forefront of Interest Films, a leadership it has held for many years and which it is determined to keep.

As regards "EVE'S FILM REVIEW" – its slogan of
"Fashion, Fun and Fancy:

briefly indicates our field – with a distinct leaning to the more feminine appeal. Incidentally, we know Adam has more than a sneaking regard for Eve's tantalising subjects that pass all too swiftly across the screen.

The latest Fashions in colour, the newest ballroom dances, each with its accompanying details freely available for all dance lovers – and their number is legion, for we had to print nearly 20,000 leaflets for one dance alone, to cope with the demand – (a wonderful exploitation point here for the Showman) interesting handicrafts, the most attractive and spectacular exhibition dances, world-famous Clubs and Cabarets, Plays, Stars on-Stage (and off-stage). Unique novelty items (such as the recent "Runaway Aeroplane") subjects appealing to the sports-women, hair-raising stunts by women, cartoons, women's industries and pastimes; Camera interviews with famous women, from world-known writers to well-known athletes, novelty films of other days, subjects for children and a thousand and one other items. All these and many others build up EVE into a most comprehensive and attractive "light" periodical and a fitting companion to its Monday release partner – the "PICTORIAL".

With Cameramen and Agents in the big centres of Paris, Berlin, New York, etc., always on the lookout for novelties – with an up-to-date central and well-equipped Studio right in the heart of the West End of London, with a highly trained technical staff, superior to any other "short" film in Britain or elsewhere, the PIC and EVE will worthily uphold the reputation of being the leaders in the Magazine or Interest film world.

They are the necessary condiments – the spice of the perfect programme, and we maintain that no programme is complete without them.

It may also interest our Salesmen to know that at the present time EVE and PICTORIAL subjects are being shown in the United States, Australia, Africa, France, Spain, Germany, Austria, Hungary and the whole of Central Europe, Holland, Switzerland, Sweden, Denmark, Norway, Egypt, the Orient, West Indies, on many Liners, in fact throughout most of the civilised world.

It would also be well to bear in mind that we were the pioneers in showing the public slow-motion photography, time-lapse flower studies, trick stop-motion, reverse action and duplicated image films, frame pictures, half-and-half underwater studies, London night scenes, Cabaret films, dance pictures with accompanying free explanatory leaflets – we were even the pioneers of illustrated titles in our endeavour to make a product as finished as possible, and we were and are the leaders in that style of titling which every other rival has striven to copy.

(1928)

Appendix 2

Pathe Cinemagazine Items Mentioned In Text

Where year of release is known it is listed. Some items are dated from stock marks (those marked with a 'c'). Films with no stock marks are dated as unknown, these items are almost certainly very early 1920s.

The EP reference number relates to the item location within Pathe's *Eve Pictorials* collection and does not correspond to original *Eve's Film Review* issue numbers.

EP 289 *After the Play is Over* (c1921) 109
EP 223 *Air Thrills for Eve* (1931) 102
EP 075 *Amusing The Youngsters* (c1921) 89
EP 001 *Annual Howlfeast, The* (1929) 95
EP 253 *Another Record-Breaker* (1933) 102
EP 020 *Are Women's Sports Too Strenuous?* (c1928) 5, 54, 99
EP 272 *Are You a Lip-Reader?* (1933) 109

EP 005 *Baseball Belles From Cardiff, The* (date unknown) 101
EP 045 *Beach Censor, The* (1925) 36
EP 218 *Beach Pebbles* (1931) 96
EP 250 *Bead Makers, The* (1932) 91
EP 191 *Beauty Exercises* (1930) 83
EP 100 *Beauty School* (c1921) 86, 87
EP 281 *Boots – Boots – Boots – Latest Russian Styles for Eve* (c1925) 47
EP 114 *Brevities* (1929) 60
EP 052 *Bridal Veils for Wedding Belles* (date unknown) 55
EP 112 *Bride of the Black Forest, The* (1929) 24
EP 055 *Buffer Belt – A Paris Novelty, The* (c1922) 36
EP 023 *Buoyant Belles – at Droitwich Spa* (date unknown) 96

EP 004 *Cameos* (1922) 135
EP 054 *Camera Interviews – Mrs Arthur Hamilton The Swimmer* (1922) 77
EP 012 *Camera Interviews – Mrs E. Macavity, The Artist* (1922) 137
EP 018 *Camera Interviews – Mrs Laura Knight* (1927) 137
EP 112 *Camera Interviews – Mlle Marise Daspie* (1929 or 1930) 137
EP 200 *Camera Interviews – Mrs Phoebe Stabler* (1930) 137
EP 286 *Camera Interviews – The Arnaut Brothers The Famous Musical Clowns* (1928) 109
EP 060 *Camisole Novelty, A* (date unknown) 47, 60
EP 078 *Can You Do These?* (c1921) 89
EP 208 *Canoe Girls of Ngaruawahia, The* (1931) 24
EP 073 *Celebrities At Home – Miss Mabel Lucie Attwell* (c1921) 137
EP 051 *Cheating the Mud Spots* (1926) 58, 135
EP 253 *Children of the Day* (1933) 95

NZFA – item is held in collection of the New Zealand Film Archive in Wellington
PT – Pathetone Weekly
SS – item is held in collection of ScreenSound Australia in Canberra

Appendix 3

Missing *Eve's Film Review* Items

This list comprises *Eve's Film Review* items known to be missing from the Pathe collection. British Pathe holds paperwork for around 350 of the 656 released *Eve's Film Review* issues. This list is therefore incomplete and should serve only as a partial guide; item titles for issues without paperwork are not known.

As an aid to identifying items the title and intertitle cards shown on p.127 are fairly typical examples. Not all intertitles and titles bear the words *Eve's Film Review* but the style of lettering remains fairly consistent throughout the 12 year run of the cinemagazine. Some title cards carry the issue number under the series title.

The EFR number relates to the issue number for the named item. This should not be confused with EP numbers which are Pathe's film can reference numbers. Paperwork does not always specify whether an item is Pathecolor (P) – this is noted where known. T A o F t C = The Adventures of Felix the Cat.

I am compiling a list of extant items in collections other than Pathe so am keen to hear from anyone who knows of the whereabouts of any of the following:

02/4/25	Advance Fashions from Paris (P) EFR 200
27/4/22	Adventures of Bud and Susie – Bud and Susie Take Up Baseball EFR 47
16/3/22	Adventures of Bud and Susie – Bud Takes the Cake EFR 41
04/5/22	Adventures of Bud and Susie – Bud & Tommy Take a Day Off EFR 48
13/4/22	Adventures of Bud and Susie – Mice – and Money EFR 45
11/6/22	Adventures of Bud and Susie – North Pole EFR 49
06/4/22	Adventures of Bud and Susie – The New Cook's Debut EFR 44
01/6/22	Adventures of Bud and Susie – The Wars of Mice and Men EFR 52
25/5/22	Adventures of Bud and Susie – They Join the "Tecs"! EFR 51
23/3/22	Adventures of Bud and Susie – Wipe Your Feet EFR 42
07/9/22	T A o F t C – A Gay Dog is Felix EFR 66
22/6/22	T A o F t C – An Awkward Customer EFR 55
30/10/24	T A o F t C – Back to the Bone Age EFR 178
31/8/22	T A o F t C – Down on the Farm EFR 65
07/2/24	T A o F t C – episode title unknown EFR 140
29/3/23	T A o F t C – episode title unknown EFR 95
29/6/22	T A o F t C – Felix and Fido's Bone EFR 56
26/6/24	T A o F t C – Felix and his Tail EFR 160
14/5/25	T A o F t C – Felix and the Fisherman EFR 206
19/6/24	T A o F t C – Felix Atones EFR 159
28/9/22	T A o F t C – Felix Becomes a Landlord EFR 69
10/1/24	T A o F t C – Felix Becomes a Nurse EFR 136
26/3/25	T A o F t C – Felix Calms his Conscience EFR 199
23/10/24	T A o F t C – Felix Comes Back EFR 177
23/4/25	T A o F t C – Felix Continues His Search EFR 203
03/7/24	T A o F t C – Felix Continues his Tail EFR 161
09/4/25	T A o F t C – Felix Done Again EFR 201
14/8/24	T A o F t C – Felix Enjoys Himself and Elopes EFR 167
15/1/25	T A o F t C – Felix Fades Away EFR 189
24/4/24	T A o F t C – Felix Falls in Love EFR 151
18/12/22	T A o F t C – Felix Finds Out EFR 185
12/3/25	T A o F t C – Felix Finishes First EFR 197
6/12/23	T A o F t C – Felix Fools Father EFR 131
06/7/22	T A o F t C – Felix Forages for Food EFR 57
21/5/25	T A o F t C – Felix Gets Broadcast EFR 207
05/3/25	T A o F t C – Felix Gets Fired EFR 196
17/7/24	T A o F t C – Felix Gets His 50/50 EFR 163

17/4/24	T A o F t C – Felix Gets Home Again EFR 150
18/9/24	T A o F t C – Felix Gets Left EFR 172
30/4/25	T A o F t C – Felix Gets Puzzled EFR 204
9/10/24	T A o F t C – Felix Gets Revenge EFR 175
16/4/25	T A o F t C – Felix – Globe Trotter EFR 202
10/4/24	T A o F t C – Felix Goes North EFR 149
12/10/22	T A o F t C – Felix Goes on Strike EFR 71
30/11/22	T A o F t C – Felix Goes to Sea EFR 78
13/3/24	T A o F t C – Felix Goes to Sea EFR 145
7/8/24	T A o F t C – Felix Goes to the Fair EFR 166
16/10/24	T A o F t C – Felix Goes West EFR 176
6/11/22	T A o F t C – Felix has a Trying Time in the Bone Age EFR 179
5/2/25	T A o F t C – Felix Has His Tail Bobbed EFR 192
28/2/24	T A o F t C – Felix Helps Shellac Homes EFR 143
6/3/24	T A o F t C – Felix Helps Shellac Homes No. 2 EFR 144
11/12/22	T A o F t C – Felix Helps the Kid EFR 184
17/8/22	T A o F t C – Felix – Hero! EFR 63
27/11/24	T A o F t C – Felix Hunts for Treasure EFR 182
05/10/22	T A o F t C – Felix – Hypnotist EFR 70
14/2/24	T A o F t C – Felix – Hypnotist EFR 141
12/2/25	T A o F t C – Felix in Fairyland EFR 193
17/1/24	T A o F t C – Felix in Love EFR 137
27/7/22	T A o F t C – Felix is a Friend in Need EFR 60
29/1/25	T A o F t C – Felix is a Ghost Getter EFR 191
1/5/24	T A o F t C – Felix is a Great Help EFR 152
11/6/25	T A o F t C – Felix is Fond of Birds EFR 210
23/11/22	T A o F t C – Felix is Left at Home EFR 77
3/1/24	T A o F t C – Felix is Still on the Move EFR 135
19/2/25	T A o F t C – Felix Joins the Circus EFR 194
24/1/24	T A o F t C – Felix Loses Out No. 2 EFR 138
24/1/24	T A o F t C – Felix Loses the Girl EFR 138
4/9/24	T A o F t C – Felix Minds the Baby EFR 170
20/7/22	T A o F t C – Felix – Nurse Girl EFR 59
24/8/22	T A o F t C – Felix on the Frolic EFR 64
28/5/25	T A o F t C – Felix On the Run EFR 208
25/12/22	T A o F t C – Felix On the Trail EFR 186
1/1/25	T A o F t C – Felix On the Trail Part 2 EFR 187
27/12/23	T A o F t C – Felix Out of Luck EFR 134
24/7/24	T A o F t C – Felix – Pole Seeker EFR 164
29/5/24	T A o F t C – Felix Puts it Over Part 1 EFR 156
5/6/24	T A o F t C – Felix Puts it Over "Tuff Tom" EFR 157
11/9/24	T A o F t C – Felix Returns the Baby EFR 171
7/5/25	T A o F t C – Felix Solves the Puzzle EFR 205
25/9/24	T A o F t C – Felix Still Chases a Meal EFR 173
20/12/23	T A o F t C – Felix Still on the Hunt EFR 133
21/6/23	T A o F t C – Felix Still Trying for Treasure EFR 107
3/4/24	T A o F t C – Felix Still Trying to Rest EFR 148
7/12/22	T A o F t C – Felix Strays Into the States EFR 79
20/3/24	T A o F t C – Felix Strays into the States EFR 146
10/7/24	T A o F t C – Felix Takes on a 50/50 Proposition EFR 162
13/11/22	T A o F t C – Felix Takes up Golf! EFR 180
21/2/24	T A o F t C – Felix Tells a Great Fish Story EFR 142
8/5/24	T A o F t C – Felix to the Rescue EFR 153
12/6/24	T A o F t C – Felix Tries for a Home EFR 158
27/3/24	T A o F t C – Felix Tries to Rest EFR 147
09/11/22	T A o F t C – Felix Turns Boxer EFR 75
14/9/22	T A o F t C – Felix Turns 'Tec EFR 67
28/8/24	T A o F t C – Felix Wakes Up EFR 169
2/4/25	T A o F t C – Felix Wants a Feed EFR 200
4/6/25	T A o F t C – Felix Wins and Loses EFR 209
26/2/25	T A o F t C – Felix Wins Out EFR 195
21/8/24	T A o F t C – Felix Yawns Along EFR 168
13/7/22	T A o F t C – Felix's Fish Story EFR 58
21/9/22	T A o F t C – Friday the 13th EFR 68
20/11/22	T A o F t C – Golf No. 2 EFR 181
22/1/25	T A o F t C – Haunted! EFR 190
13/12/23	T A o F t C – He Goes Hunting EFR 132
2/10/24	T A o F t C – He's in Trouble Again EFR 174
15/5/24	T A o F t C – Helping a Farmer EFR 154
08/6/22	T A o F t C – Introducing a Hungry Little Fellow EFR 53
26/10/22	T A o F t C – Out of Luck EFR 73
16/11/22	T A o F t C – The Free Lunch Fellow EFR 76
19/3/25	T A o F t C – The Interloper! EFR 198
14/6/23	T A o F t C – The Treasure Hunters EFR 106
3/8/22	T A o F t C – The Villain Intrudeth EFR 61
8/1/25	T A o F t C – They Said it with Ukeleles! EFR 188
Various 1923	Adventures of Peggy (Series of 9 featuring Peggy Hyland – all missing) Various
21/2/24	The Air Line EFR 143

126

(103) Example of a title card –
Eve's Little Extravagences

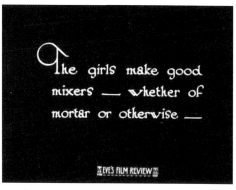

(104) Example of an intertitle card –
The Lady Bricklayers

(104) The End Credit –
East Anglian Film Archive

Appendix 4

Eve's Film Review Items Viewable on the Pathe Website

British Pathe intends to make its entire collection viewable over the internet in the next few years.

Until then Pathe have made a selection of *Eve's Film Review* items available to view at www.britishpathe.com/all_about_eve.htm

EP 253	*Another Record-Breaker* (1933)
EP 020	*Are Women's Sports Too Strenuous?* (c1928)
EP 054	*Camera Interviews – Mrs Arthur Hamilton The Swimmer* (1922)
EP 193	*Citrus* (1930)
EP 233	*Crowning Glories!* (1932)
EP 076	*F-A-S-H-I-O-N and How Eve Spells It – an Idare Fantasy* (1922)
EP 250	*Nerve!* (1932)
EP 025	*Parisian Capes and Shapes* (date unknown)
EP 093	*Scotland v Russia* (1926)
EP 238	*Seeing Sights in the Sierras* (1932)
EP 214	*Terpsichore* (1930)
EP 250	*The Bead Makers* (1932)
EP 099	*The Flat Charleston Made Easy* (1927)
EP 218	*The Massage Robot* (1931)
EP 114	*The Rival* (1930)
EP 237	*The Weigh of All Flesh* (Eliminator!) (1932)
EP 045	*We Go to Coventry! – And the Reason Why* (1927)
EP 239	*Where My Caravan Is Rested 2* (1932)

Notes for Chapter One – Three Girls in a Boat

1. *British Newsreel Issue Sheets 1913-1970: the complete collection held by the Slade Film History Register reproduced on microfiche* (Graphic Data Publishing/British Universities Film and Video Council, 1984). This extremely useful resource comprises lists of items released in various British newsreels and cinemagazines. The British Universities Film and Video Council has since expanded on this work by compiling a searchable database featuring descriptions of many newsreel and cinemagazine items. This is available on CD-ROM and via the B.U.F.V.C. website at: www.bufvc.ac.uk

2. The following apology appeared on page 21 of the *Picturegoer* magazine of 14 January 1922: 'Sorry! Our Mistake. In the article Filming Fashions, which appeared in our December 17 issue, *Eve's Film Review* was referred to as Eve's Pictorial, quite a good alternative title, but 'Eve' prefers to be known as a Film Review. This latest and most popular Pathé animated journal is a much-sought-after treat to feminine 'fans'. Besides fashions, it deals with almost every subject dear to the heart of the fair sex.'

3. When *Eve's Film Review* was launched a £50 prize was offered to any lady patron who could propose a suitable alternative title for the weekly women's film. A short film a few weeks later informed the audience that: 'No alternative title sufficiently outstanding to warrant us changing that of *Eve's Film Review* was suggested'. The prize money was shared between five women whose efforts were considered the best but *Eve's Film Review* continued to be the cinemagazine's official title – unfortunately there are no records of the alternative titles suggested.

4. Tony Fletcher has evidence of Pathe producing some sound *Eve's Film Review* items in 1929. I have found no sound items from this period and it seems that Pathe decided to produce a new cinemagazine (*Pathetone Weekly*) rather than turn *Eve's Film Review* into a sound reel. The only *Eve's Film Review* item I have discovered with sound, *Tinycraft* from 1931 seems to be an anomaly. Pathe occasionally produced sound and silent versions of the same story in the early 1930s but normally the sound version would be produced for the *Pathetone Weekly* or *Pathe Pictorial*. *Eve's Film Review* continued to be produced as a 'silent' cinemagazine until 1933.

5. Articles which mention Ken Gordon working on *Eve's Film Review* include **Filming Palm Beach: Some of the Trials of a Cameraman's Life**, *Kinematograph Weekly* 17 June 1926 p 72 and **Famous Club Filmed – Pathe's Big Scoop for *Eve's Film Review***, *Kinematograph Weekly* 21 January 1926 p 58. The latter reports on Pathe's filming of the item *Famous Clubs And Cabarets No 1. The Kit Cat Club*.

6. Little is known about Edward Eve's time at Pathe. He is not mentioned in any company records but his son remembers him working at the company in the 1920s and 1930s. In the 1940s and 1950s he directed feature films through his own company "Edward Eve Productions". I am indebted both to Jim Ballantyne and John Eve for providing information about Edward Eve.

7. This quote is from a typewritten press release entitled **Just 'Pic and Eve' by Editor Watts**. It is a fascinating insight into the aims of the editor of the *Pathe Pictorial* and *Eve's Film Review* and can be found in full as Appendix 1. The press release was written in response to a memo from a Mr Judge of First National Pathe Limited dated 24 October 1928 asking Mr Watts to write an article on the production policy of the two cinemagazines. Some of this material was used in a much later article: **World's Best Variety Talent in Pathe Periodicals**, *Kinematograph Weekly* 14 November 1935 p 25.

Notes for Chapter Two – The Arrival of The Women's Film

1. Iris Barry, *Let's Go to the Pictures* (Chatto & Windus, 1926) p 59.
2. Marjory Williams, **The Woman Patron**, *Kine Weekly* 3 December 1925 p 47.
3. *Eastern Daily Press* 7 September 1925 p 6.
4. Mike Hammond is a lecturer in the English department at the University of Southampton. This work is part of his unpublished PhD Thesis 'The Big Show: British Cinema and Reception During the Great War'. Nottingham Trent University, 2001.

5. Quoted by Pamela Horn, *Women in the 1920s* (Alan Sutton Publishing, 1995) p 184. The original source of the quote is unclear.
6. Luke McKernan suggests that the first cinemagazine for women was probably the *Kinemacolor Fashion Gazette*. This was produced in 1913 and only ran for a few issues. No examples are known to survive. From contemporary reports the reel seemed to be solely concerned with fashion and did not have the scope or longevity of *Eve's Film Review*. Interestingly, it was edited by a woman, Abby Meehan. Not much is known about Ms Meehan – a subject for further research.
7. This review was quoted in Elizabeth Leese, *Costume Design in the Movies: An Illustrated Guide to the Work of 157 Great Designers* (Dover Publications, 1991) p 9. Exact date and page reference for the original source was not given.
8. I am extremely grateful to David Francis of the Library of Congress for showing me two *Eve's Film Review* posters from his personal collection and allowing me to reproduce one here. Before David produced these from a suitcase to show me, I had no idea that the reels were advertised in such a way and was thrilled to see what must surely be extremely rare examples of these fabulous posters.
9. The image of a scandalised old-fashioned woman in the *Eve's Film Review* launch advertisement: **3** foreshadows this.

Notes for Chapter Three – Fashion Fun and Fancy

1. **Hints to the Programme Builder**, *Kinematograph Weekly Newsreels and Shorts Supplement* 28 March 1926 p 3.
2. Pathe often claimed that their *Pathe Pictorial* was the first cinemagazine. In fact there had been other irregular cinemagazines such as *Screen-Magazine* produced by a company called Trans-Atlantic. It seems however that the *Pictorial* was the first British cinemagazine to be produced every week.
3. Details from a programme for the Piccadilly Cinema, Manchester of 2nd April 1923 held in the British Film Institute Library. Reference: BFI Special Collections – Cinema Ephemera: Regions/Manchester Piccadilly Picture Theatre.
4. There is a possibility that overseas exhibitors screened items from several different production companies spliced together in one reel. The New Zealand Film Archive in Wellington has a stencil coloured *Eve's Film Review* item called *Paris Fashions in Advance* within a reel which also included *Topical Budget* and *Pathe Gazette* items. It is equally possible however that the items were spliced together at a later date by a film collector.
5. Advertisements for this Norwich cinema in the *Eastern Daily Press* regularly mentioned both cinemagazines as well as the main feature during October 1925. The Regent Cinema in Norwich was also showing *Eve's Film Review* at this time.
6. **Just 'Pic and Eve' by Editor Watts** – see Appendix 1.
7. Ibid.
8. In a letter to the author dated 24 August 1995.
9. Extract from transcript number: T95-18 quoted in: Annette Kuhn, **Memories of Cinema-going in the 1930s**, *Journal of Popular British Cinema* Issue 2 – 1999 p 102. The transcriptions attempt to convey a sense of the interviewees' voices so regional pronunciations are spelt phonetically.
10. **Illuminating Response to Bernstein Questionnaire**, *The Bioscope* 4 August 1927 p 20. It seems that this question would have included cinemagazines and short 'interest' films in the term 'news' pictures as other questions in the survey related to the feature film.
11. Kuhn, **Memories of Cinema-going in the 1930s**, *Journal of Popular British Cinema* p 103.
12. Jim Ballantyne of the British Universities Film and Video Council in a letter to the author dated 20 December 1993.
13. *Motion Picture Herald* New York 26 May 1945, quoted in: Peter Baechlin and Maurice Muller-Strauss, *Newsreels Across the World* (U.N.E.S.C.O., 1952) p 30.
14. D.F. Taylor, **Screen Magazines**, *Cinema Quarterly* Winter 1933-4 p 93.
15. Quoted in: Luke McKernan, *Topical Budget: The Great British News Film* (British Film Institute, 1992) p 121.
16. Intertitle from *Eyelashes While You Wait*.
17. *Musical Dog – British Movietone News*, 2nd December 1929 ('Canine prodigy conducts jazz orchestra rendering popular tune. Alsatian dog stands on hind legs and conducts'),

Wrestling with a Lion – *British Movietone News*, 27th March 1930 ('Twisting a lion's tail for fun. Californian wrestler is thrown after big battle. Shots of the wrestling') and *Patterns made in the water by 64 German ladies* – *Universal News*, 9th February 1931. All descriptions from the British Universities Film and Video Council's CD-ROM entitled 'British Universities Newsreel Project' – no description found for the German ladies story.

18. Baechlin and Muller-Strauss, *Newsreels Across the World* p 19.
19. *Topical Budget* issue 732 reviewed in: **The Week's Short Stuff**, *Kinematograph Weekly* 10 September 1925 p 29.
20. **Short Features**, *The Bioscope* 15 August 1928 p 40.
21. Andrew Buchanan, *Films, The Way of the Cinema* (Pitman, 1932) p 197. Andrew Buchanan was the producer of the *Ideal Cinemagazine* which ran from 1926 to 1938.
22. **Just 'Pic and Eve' by Editor Watts** – see Appendix 1.
23. An interesting link between the 'serious' documentary makers and the 'non-serious' cinemagazine makers can be seen in a letter in the Pathe correspondence file from Frederick Watts (editor of Pathe cinemagazines) to Major Creighton of the Empire Marketing Board. An extract reads:
    'Very many thanks for your kind remarks regarding our work for you. We are very pleased to hear it has proved so satisfactory. I trust to have the pleasure of doing more work for you in the near future, which you may rest assured will have my personal attention.'
    The letter is dated 30 October 1929 so it seems that the Empire Marketing Board used the same team that made the 'frivolous' cinemagazine to make films for propaganda purposes before establishing their own documentary film-making department.
24. Buchanan, **Screen Magazines**, *The Way of the Cinema* p 187.
25. Taylor, **Screen Magazines**, *Cinema Quarterly* p 93.
26. Ibid. p 93. That cinemagoers might not appreciate this attempt to 'improve' them is hinted at in Leslie Halliwell's autobiography. Speaking of a cinemagazine which attempted to deal with the serious issues of the day, his reminiscences read as follows:
    '*The March of Time* came in with a flourish of critical acclaim, but at twenty minutes it seemed dry and overlong to us, telling us things we did not want to know about countries of which we had scarcely heard. What we did enjoy about it, for we then knew that the endurance test was over, was the spontaneous chorus which rose from stalls and circle alike to echo the commentator's last portentous 'Time Marches On'.'
    Leslie Halliwell, *Seats in All Parts: Half a Lifetime at the Movies* (Granada Publishing Ltd, 1985) p 49.
27. **Just 'Pic and Eve' by Editor Watts** – see Appendix 1.
28. Tom Gunning, **The Cinema of Attractions: Early Film, its Spectator and the Avant-Garde**, in Thomas Elsaesser (Ed), *Early Cinema: Space – Frame – Narrative* (British Film Institute, 1990) pp 56-62.
29. Ibid. p 57.
30. Tom Gunning, **An Unseen Energy Swallows Space: The Space in Early Film and its Relation to America** in John L. Fell (Ed), *Film Before Griffith* (University of California Press, 1983) p 359.
31. **World's Best Variety Talent in** *Pathe Pictorials*, *Kinematograph Weekly* 14 November 1935 p 25.
32. The hugely popular cartoon character Felix the Cat made its first screen appearance in Britain as a regular segment of *Eve's Film Review*.
33. Nick Hiley's article **Let's Go To The Pictures: The British Cinema Audience in the 1920s and 1930s**, *The Journal of Popular British Cinema* Issue 2 – 1999 pp 39-53 provides much fascinating information about cinemagoing habits in the period. Interesting to note here is the gradual change from a large number of small venues showing films in the early 1920s (including theatres and music halls) to a smaller number of large purpose built cinemas in the early 1930s. The year *Eve's Film Review* ceased production – 1933 – is mentioned in the text as a year in which hundreds of cheaper and smaller venues were forced to close as they could not compete with the larger picture palaces offering the latest sound technology.

Notes for Chapter Four – Powder Puff Culture

1. *The Express* 12th November 1924 quoted in: Billie Melman, *Women and the Popular Imagination in the Twenties: Flappers and Nymphs* (Macmillan, 1988) p 23.
2. Ibid. p 18.
3. Clemence Dane **Two Million Women**, *Britannia and Eve* May 1929 p 20.
4. *Punch* 30 November 1927 p 591 quoted by Melman, *Women and the Popular Imagination in the Twenties: Flappers and Nymphs* p 29.
5. Figures quoted by Noreen Branson, *Britain in the Nineteen Twenties* (Weiderfeld and Nicolson, 1975) p 203.
6. *Daily Mail* 20 April 1927 quoted in: Branson, *Britain in the Nineteen Twenties* p 203. The Equal Franchise Act gave all women over 21 the vote in 1928.
7. Helena Normanton, **Do Men Want Women in Politics?**, *Good Housekeeping* October 1926. Quoted in: Brian Braithwaite, Noelle Walsh and Glyn Davies (Eds), *Ragtime to Wartime: The Best of Good Housekeeping 1922-1939* (Ebury Press, 1986) p 29.
8. Irene Clephane, *Towards Sex Freedom* (John Lane, 1935) pp 200-1. Quoted in Pamela Horn, *Women in the 1920s* (Alan Sutton Publishing, 1995) p 16.
9. Intertitle from the film *Is Eve Going Too Far – In Athletics?*
10. This item is one of many within *Eve's Film Review* where a modern interpretation might be at odds with what the film's connotations would have been at the time. Although not obvious to modern audiences, the device that is demonstrated is probably an aid to learning the correct distance between bodies when performing a particular ballroom dance. However, the intertitle 'Every day in every way Continental dances get closer and closer, so the Paris Eves have just started "Buffer States" of their own' suggests that the allusion to keeping a man at bay would have been clear to 1920s viewers too.
11. Timothy Charlesworth **Our Super Women**, *Eve the Lady's Pictorial* 16 January 1929 p 103.
12. Melman, *Women and the Popular Imagination in the Twenties: Flappers and Nymphs* p 42.
13. Ros Ballaster, Margaret Beetham, Elizabeth Frazer and Sandra Hebron, *Women's Worlds: Ideology, Femininity and the Woman's Magazine* (Macmillan, 1991) p 124.
14. In 1920 **The Letters of Eve** transferred to *Pan* magazine where it was illustrated first by Jo White and then by Dolly Tree.
15. **The Letters of Eve**, *The Tatler* 20 August 1919 p 226. *Eve* was a sister magazine to *The Tatler* – they shared a publisher and probably the same editor. The text of **The Letters of Eve** feature was written by Mrs Maitland Davies. It has been suggested that Barbara Cartland also contributed to this column; the Crusader in Pink was considered to be one of the 'bright young things' of the 1920s.
16. Anne Harriet Fish contributed cartoons to many newspapers and magazines of the 1910s and 1920s. The three books inspired by **The Letters of Eve** were attributed to 'Fish and Fowl', Fowl being the nom de plume of the editor of *The Tatler* Edward Huskinson. The *Adventures of Eve* series was produced by Gaumont in 1918 and 1919.
17. Although affordable by many, it was one of the more expensive magazines on the newsstands. (The average weekly wage for a Staffordshire pottery worker in 1920, for instance, was £2.43 – approx 50 shillings).
18. Male writers for women's magazines of the period included Godfrey Winn and Beverley Nichols.
19. *Eve* November 1919 p 1.
20. Edward Huskinson was probably the editor of *Eve the Lady's Pictorial* at its launch. Philip Ziegler mentions that Lady Diana Cooper was offered the job of editress-in-chief at some stage of the magazine's history. Ziegler states that she turned the job down because she didn't like the chairman of the Illustrated Newspaper Group who published the magazine. Philip Ziegler, *The Biography of Lady Diana Cooper* (Penguin Books, 1981) p 192.
21. Ballaster, *Women's Worlds: Ideology, Femininity and the Woman's Magazine* p 11.
22. Advertisement for Abdullah cigarettes, *Britannia and Eve* May 1929 p 8.
23. **Eve in Paradise**, *Eve* December 1919 p 9. The title of this regular article can be read both as 'Eve in Paradise' and 'Eve in Paris', as the final word is transcribed in two different typefaces.
24. If there was a weekly programme on television today called *Cosmopolitan Television Magazine* which covered the same topics as the print magazine *Cosmopolitan*, I know I would assume that the two were linked.

25. *Eve the Lady's Pictorial* merged with *Britannia* magazine in 1929. Before this time *Britannia* was a magazine which dealt mostly with politics, influential men (military personalities, 'captains of industry' etc.) and men's sports. After merging with *Eve the Lady's Pictorial* the magazine became 'feminised' with articles on female fashions, housekeeping and women's sports alongside its more traditionally 'masculine' features.
26. Advertisement with subtitle **The Jottings of Joan – The Ladies' Club, Harrods, SW**, *Eve* December 1919 p v.
27. Advertisement for Haig Whisky *Britannia and Eve* May 1929 p 155.
28. Advertisement for Heals *Eve* 18th March 1920 p i.
29. Jeanne Thomas Allen, *"Fig Leaves"* in Hollywood: Female Representation and Consumer Culture in Jane Gaines and Charlotte Herzog (Eds), *Fabrications: Costume and the Female Body* (Routledge, 1990) pp 126-7.
30. **Criticisms of the Films**, *The Bioscope* 19 August 1926 p 33.
31. Intertitle from: *The Stars As They Are – Miss Evelyn Laye*.
32. **Style Police: Snakeskin**, *Reality, The Independent on Sunday* 23 April 2000 p 31.
33. Intertitle from an *Eve's Film Review* item called *Cameos*, which features accessories such as large silk flowers attached to waistbands, and headbands with dangling bunches of grapes attached.
34. Statistic quoted by Alan Jenkins, *The Thirties* (Heinemann, 1976) p 36. He does not list the references for the original source.
35. There is always an exception that proves the rule and within *Eve's Film Review* there are two. The first is a film called *The Pruner's Progress*. Amongst shots of a woman pruning an apple tree and (naturally) eating an apple, intertitles read: 'Somehow, Eve always **did** like apples… But only through the labour saving "Plucca" Pruner, made by the Elliott Pruner Co., 19, Regent St., London, will she have a plentiful supply next year'. The second example mentions a company in the film's title: *Eve Buys A Camera From Soho Ltd*. These are the only examples I have seen of explicit advertising within *Eve's Film Review* where cinemagoers were told where they could buy a particular item.
36. K. Sawchuk, **A tale of inscription/fashion statements** in *Body Invaders: Panic Sex in America* (St Martins, 1987) p 64. Quoted by Jennifer Craik, *The Face of Fashion: Cultural Studies in Fashion* (Routledge, 1994) pp.46-7.
37. Julia Kristeva, *About Chinese Women* (Marion Boyars, 1977) p 38. Quoted by Lorraine Gamman in **Watching the Detectives: The Enigma of the Female Gaze,** in Lorraine Gamman and Margaret Marshment (Eds), *The Female Gaze* (The Women's Press, 1988) p 17.
38. Intertitle from *The Rival Sex*.

Notes for Chapter Five – For Ladies Only – Adam May Glance

1. *For Ladies Only* is the title of an *Eve's Film Review* item. Immediately following the main title is the subtitle 'Adam may glance'.
2. C.A. Lejeune, *Cinema* (A. Maclehose & Co. 1931) p 213.
3. Laura Mulvey, **Visual Pleasure and Narrative Cinema,** *Screen* 16:3 Autumn 1975 p 8.
4. John Berger, *Ways of Seeing* (Penguin Books, 1972) p 51.
5. Ibid. p 46.
6. Mulvey, **Visual Pleasure and Narrative Cinema**, *Screen* p 11.
7. **Just 'Pic and Eve' by Editor Watts** – see Appendix 1.
8. Intertitle from *Eve's Film Review* item *Cheating the Mud Spots*.
9. Sigmund Freud, **Fetishism**, *On Sexuality: Three Essays on the Theory of Sexuality and Other Works* (Penguin, 1977) p 355.
10. First intertitle from *Paris Frocks For Autumn*, second from *Paris Fashions in Advance*.
11. Constance Balides, **Scenarios of exposure in the practice of everyday life: women in the cinema of attractions**, *Screen* 34:1 Spring 1993 pp 19-37.
12. I would hazard a guess that *Citrus* and *Seeing Sights in the Sierras* were shot by the same cameraman. Not only are they very similar stylistically, I think I recognise the chorine in the last shot of *Seeing Sights in the Sierras* sitting on the orange cart in *Citrus*.
13. **Pathés Novelty Show**, *The Film Renter and Moving Picture News* 18 June 1921 p 35.
14. Rosalind Coward, *Female Desires: How they are Sought, Bought and Packaged* (Paladin, 1984) p 57.

15. Exceptions to this are the theatrical items and dance routines. However, these are almost without fail filmed from a static camera position without point-of-view shots. Thus although there are men on-screen in these items, they are not filmed in accordance with "classical narrative cinema"conventions.
16. Tom Gunning, **What I Saw from the Rear Window of the Hotel des Folies-Dramatiques, Or the Story Point-of-View Films Told**, in André Gaudrealt (Ed), *Ce que je vois de mon ciné...* (Meridiens Klincksieck, 1988) quoted in: Miriam Hansen, *Babel and Babylon: Spectatorship in American Silent Film* (Harvard University Press, 1991) p 40.
17. Joe Noble.
18. Mary Ann Doane, **Film and the Masquerade: Theorising the Female Spectator**, *Screen* 23:3-4, 1982 p 77.
19. Judith Mayne, **Uncovering the Female Body**, in John L. Fell (Ed), *Before Hollywood: Turn of the Century American Film* (Hudson Hills Press, 1987) p 66.
20. Hansen, *Babel and Babylon: Spectatorship in American Silent Film* p 39.
21. Ibid. p 39.
22. Intertitle from *Where My Caravan Has Rested 2*.
23. Jackie Stacey, *Star-gazing: Hollywood Cinema and Female Spectatorship* (Routledge, 1991).
24. Mulvey, **Visual Pleasure and Narrative Cinema**, *Screen* p 12.
25. Camille Paglia, *Sex, Art and American Culture* (Vintage Books, 1992) p 288.
26. Jane Gaines paraphrasing Carol Ascher in: **Introduction: Fabricating the Female Body** Jane Gaines and Charlotte Herzog (Eds), *Fabrications: Costume and the Female Body* (Routledge, 1990) p 6.
27. Paglia, *Sex, Art and American Culture* p 288.

Notes for Chapter Six – An Overview of the Films

1. Intertitle from *Tea Gowns (And That's Not All) of Worth*. Full intertitle reads: 'Who does Eve dress for? Herself or Adam? While Adam thinks it out, Eve can examine this brocade charmeuse gown, with ostrich feathers to match'. This is a 'missing' Pathecolor item, the intertitle has been transcribed from paper records.
2. From paper records it seems that each *Eve's Film Review* issue featured at least one Pathecolor (stencil colour) item. No stencil colour prints of *Eve's Film Review* items survive at Pathe, although the collection does include a few *Pathe Pictorial* travelogue items from this period in Pathecolor. It seems that although Pathe kept nitrate negatives of many of their early productions, prints were not systematically archived until the 1950s. However, many national film archives around the world have examples of colour *Eve's Film Review* prints. A particularly good collection exists at the Australian film archive ScreenSound Australia. Colour fashion items seem to have been the most likely *Eve's Film Review* items to be kept by collectors and acquired by archives. Non Pathecolor items were tinted and toned – some colour information is noted in the Pathe files. Of the *Eve's Film Review* prints I have seen in other archives, all have had coloured intertitles – pink naturally! For details of film colouring, see: Brian Coe, *The History of Movie Photography* (Ash and Grant, 1981).
3. **Studying Fashion on the Film**, *The Film Renter and Moving Picture News* 21 May 1921 p B.
4. Intertitle from *Ladies Prefer Furs. Some Latest British Fur Fashions*.
5. At least I have never seen one. There are around 1000 silent *Pathe Pictorial* stories in the Pathe library and none are serious fashion stories. The Leslie Henson film is the only item to touch on fashion.
6. Intertitle from *Shadow Shrinking Exercises – No. 2*.
7. Intertitle from *Paper Millinery – While You Wait*.
8. So far I have not been able to find an example of one of these leaflets despite scouring junk shops and the internet. Let me know if you find one!
9. Intertitle from *Italy's Land Girls*.
10. I am thinking here in particular of *It* (1927) starring Clara Bow, *Show People* (1928) with Marion Davies, and Louise Brooks in *Prix de Beaute (1930)*. Obviously not all films of the period used this 'working girl does good' storyline but the Cinderella fairy tale narrative was undoubtedly popular with female audiences of the period under consideration here.
11. Pamela Horn's excellent book *Women in The 1920s* (Alan Sutton Publishing, 1995) holds much fascinating information about the lives of women during the post war period. From census information she has deduced that 78 per cent of the female labour force were single

in 1921. The figure of women employed in the cluster of traditional jobs listed here was 71.1 per cent in 1921 and 71.6 ten years later.

12. Intertitle from *Cuddles – Filmed at Margate*.
13. Films referred to are: *Camera Interviews – Mrs E. Macavity, The Artist*; *Celebrities At Home – Miss Mabel Lucie Attwell*; *The Stars At Home – Miss May Moore-Duprez*; and *The Dancing Lesson*.
14. Full intertitle from *The Seaside Eves* reads: 'They're love-like, And dove-like, They're Angels from above-like, They're the joyous little Eves By the glad sea waves.'
15. Intertitle from *Water Witches*.
16. Intertitle from *Eve Takes Up Baseball*.
17. Intertitle from *Camera Interviews – Mlle Marise Daspie*. Pathe got the name of this aviatrix wrong – the woman who appears in the film is probably Maryse Bastie although her name is given as Marise Daspie in the film's title.
18. This film is an outstanding example of the care taken by film makers over these short subjects. Although not true in every case, in general *Eve's Film Review* items are well crafted with good lighting, editing and framing. Time was obviously taken to make the films look good – they were definitely not just cheap 'fillers'.
19. Joan Lowell features in the film *Sailor Girl*.
20. Intertitle from *Hope (New Edition)*.
21. It is possible that the woman featured was 'daredevil cowgirl' Vera McGinnis – see *Cowgirls* by Candace Savage (Bloomsbury Publishing, 1996).
22. Films referred to are: *Camera Interviews – Mrs Laura Knight* and *Camera Interviews – Mrs Phoebe Stabler*.
23. Intertitle from *Something New in Cabarets*.
24. Barrie Oliver appears in several *Eve's Film Review* items but the one I am thinking of here is *London's Famous Clubs And Cabarets No. 2 – 'Playtime At The Piccadilly'*. This is also the film which featured 'Hank the Mule'. Evon Pinard (I believe this is the correct spelling of her name) was also known as 'The Woman in Bronze'. She appears in *Producing a Cabaret Show*.
25. Some of the acts probably approached Pathe asking to be filmed – others were hand picked. For example, there is a letter in the Pathe files inviting 'Miss Tamara' to visit the Pathe Studios in 1928. A Pathe employee had seen her performing at the Wood Green Empire and obviously liked the look of her!
26. Although named as Mildred Melrose by Pathe it is quite possible that the dancer is actually Muriel Melrose who danced in Andre Charlot revues and at the Piccadilly Hotel cabaret. Pathe occasionally misspelt names in their intertitles and title sequences.
27. Although named in intertitle as 'Chaz' this comedian may be Chas Chase who was later famous for his 'Monsieur Mangetout' style routines – eating everything in sight.
28. Films referred to are: *Mr Harry Tate – At Home, Stars at Home – Billy Merson the Well Known Comedian, Stars at Home – Nellie Wallace, The Stars As They Are – Lorna and Toots Pounds, The Stars As They Are – Miss Madge Saunders and Mr Leslie Henson* and *The Stars As They Are – Miss Evelyn Laye*.
29. Dancers in gymslips are featured in *Steps! From "Good News" At The Carlton Theatre, London*. The ice-skating chorus girls are seen in *London's Famous Clubs & Cabarets – C.B. Cochran's Trocadero Cabaret 'And So We Go On'* and the fig leafed girls appear in *Legs – A Joe Noble Cartoon Survey*.

Notes for Chapter Seven – An Adamless Eden

1. *The Film Renter and Moving Picture News* 28 May 1921 pp 4-5. There was a 'spoof' reel called *Adam's Film Review* made by Harry Hughes in 1924. It seems that this was a one off pastiche in the same vein as *The Pathetic Gazette* made by Adrian Brunel. *Adam's Film Review* – alas – is 'missing believed lost'.
2. Wendy Lesser, *His Other Half: Men Looking at Women Through Art* (Harvard University Press, 1991) p 4.
3. *The Film Renter and Moving Picture News* 2 December 1922 p 67.

INDEX